T0197178

# Wings of
# *Gold*
# Wings of
# *Truth*

# Wings of
# *Gold*
# Wings of
# *Truth*

## William "Fritz" Klumpp

WESTBOW
PRESS®
A DIVISION OF THOMAS NELSON
& ZONDERVAN

WestBow Press books may be ordered through booksellers or by contacting:

WestBow Press
A Division of Thomas Nelson & Zondervan
1663 Liberty Drive
Bloomington, IN 47403
www.westbowpress.com
1 (866) 928-1240

ISBN: 978-1-9736-6538-0 (sc)
ISBN: 978-1-9736-6540-3 (hc)
ISBN: 978-1-9736-6539-7 (e)

Library of Congress Control Number: 2019907032

Print information available on the last page.

WestBow Press rev. date: 8/15/2019

# PREFACE

"Joe, we've been hit".

"It's not the flak you see that you need to be concerned about", they said, "it's the flak you don't see that you need to worry about." I had not seen anything but the target, but the red lights on my cockpit warning panel told me that the bump we felt was more than clear air turbulence. In one instant my life could dramatically change. The words of William Ernest Hensley's Invictus which I had chosen as my life's verse, "I am the master of my fate, I am the captain of my soul" had come to an inglorious end. "Please God, if you're there help me. I don't want to be a POW, and I sure would like to see my wife and my two little girls again."

Thirty-six years later it was "Survivors' Weekend" in Midland, Michigan. My dear friend Marc Smith, who was the youngest plant manager ever to reach such a position at Dow Chemical, had been instrumental in starting a CBMC committee in Midland and was active in his church. CBMC is an organization that was started in Chicago during The Great Depression, a time when men who had lost everything they had invested their lives in were jumping out of tall buildings. A group of businessmen who had found meaning and purpose that transcended the stock market banded together to share what they had determined to be the best news in life.

Marc arranged for me to speak at a luncheon on Friday and then to speak at three separate services at his former church on

Sunday morning. The weekend was titled "Survivors Weekend ", and in addition to my sharing my personal story as "a survivor", a beautiful young lady and mother of three who had lost her eyesight was scheduled to sing. Since there was nothing scheduled for Saturday, we planned to visit a maximum-security prison where the singer would lead off and I would then share my personal story.

When we arrived at the prison, we began the lengthy process of gaining entrance. I remembered well the time that I desperately feared becoming a prisoner, and now I was going through all this procedure to get inside; how ironic.

Upon completing the check-in, we were led through the yard, several inner areas, and then into the gymnasium. The inmates soon followed, and as they filed into the bleachers I wondered, "How are any of these guys going to be able to relate to anything I have to say?" They were a motley crew, to say the least and not the type I would want to meet alone in a dark alley of any city.

After the singer had completed one of her songs, I stood before this colorful group of "lifers" and began to share my story. I glanced up into the stands and it initially appeared that my audience didn't even want to sit too close to each other. They did, however, seem to be listening, and about halfway through my message, a large black man in one of the rear rows leaned forward and looked to be in tears.

When I finished speaking, the men came forward one by one with comments of appreciation. Some thanked me for my military service and for defending our country. Others just thanked me for sharing my story. One had scribbled a favorite Bible verse on a scrap of paper and another shared that he was from Jacksonville, Florida; his only wish was simply to visit his hometown one more time before he died.

I tell this story because of the impact this experience had on me personally. It was indeed profound. As I thought about what had transpired and the men I met in that prison, I realized it was solely by God's sovereign will that I was born at the time and in the place that I was. But, by the grace of God, I was not born the illegitimate son of an unmarried, minority mom addicted to crack cocaine in inner-city Detroit. The time and circumstances of my arrival were events over which I had absolutely no control.

# Wings Of
# *Gold*

# CHAPTER 1

## *In the Beginning*

Psalm 139:13-16 (ESV)

For you formed my inward parts;
  you knitted me together in my mother's womb.
<sup>14</sup> I praise you, for I am fearfully and wonderfully made.
Wonderful are your works;
  my soul knows it very well.
<sup>15</sup> My frame was not hidden from you,
when I was being made in secret,
  intricately woven in the depths of the earth.
<sup>16</sup> Your eyes saw my unformed substance;
in your book were written, every one of them,
  the days that were formed for me,
  when as yet there was none of them.

I entered this world on July 2, 1939, the second child and first son of Frederick Herman and Lidie-Adele Pittman Klumpp. The year I was born was also the year Freddie and Lidie moved into their new home on Brockenbraugh Court in Metairie, Louisiana, with me and my older sister Jean Carol. Jean was a year and a half my senior. My brother Charlie was born three and a half years later, and my youngest brother, Michael, was born when I was sixteen. That Cape Cod cottage would be my home for my first seventeen years. Growing up on Brockenbraugh Court in the forties and fifties in many respects represented an ideal childhood.

I was too young to understand the full implications of World War II in which the United States became involved when I was two years old. Dad, who was ineligible for the draft, became an air raid warden, so I do remember the air raids as we huddled in the living room and ensured that all the lights were out. I also remember victory gardens, rationing coupons, and especially the celebrations on Victory Day. The United States had liberated Europe from Nazi Germany and defeated Japan, and those victories made it a time when the entire nation could be proud to be American.

Our family wasn't the family of Ozzie and Harriet, for we had our own dysfunctions. But I never questioned my parents' love for their offspring. Dad worked hard, perhaps some would say too hard. His real estate business kept him busy even on weekends, and there wasn't time on his calendar or room in his emotional space for one-on-one time with his sons. Neither my mother nor my dad attended church except at Christmas or Easter. They were good, kind-hearted people, and thanks to my dad, all of his children inherited his strong work ethic, a strong sense of integrity, and an understanding of the value of community service.

Although mom and dad didn't attend church, they packed their three children off to Sunday School every Sunday. Sunday School, for us, was not an option until we entered our later high school years. I developed an appreciation for our nation's Judeo-Christian values and although much of what I heard became nothing more than Christian clichés, I never questioned the existence of a Supreme Being.

Early on I discovered that when I did something good, I gained praise and approval. This led me to develop a sense of value or self-worth based on my performance. While seeking affirmation is not entirely bad for a child, it may distort one's image and make him dependent upon others' opinions for his feelings of acceptance and self-esteem.

In church and Sunday school, people often spoke of a person's soul. My young mind envisioned the soul as an organ similar to one's heart or liver. Although my soul was initially clean or white, every time I did something bad, my soul would be darkened by a black spot. In turn, every time I did something good that black spot would turn white again. If my soul remained mostly white, when I died my soul would be acceptable to God and I would go to heaven. The trick then was to ensure that every time I did something bad, I had to be sure to do two good things. This way I could cancel out the black, keeping my soul white and acceptable to God. We also learned the Ten Commandments, and although later I could not recite them, the Ten Commandments and the Golden Rule became for me a standard of right and wrong.

My father and his brother had both graduated from a small military day school, New Orleans Academy, in the uptown section of New Orleans. I began 5th grade at this very school. During that same year I wrote an essay about wanting to go to the Naval Academy. I have no idea where this thought originated other than the fact that Mother and Dad both talked of a military career as being an honorable profession. They were very patriotic, and their influence, as well as the patriotism reinforced at school, led me to believe that service to God and country and a career in the military could provide an exciting and meaningful life. These values and ideas were strengthened by some of my early readings, such as *Captains Courageous* and the *Horatio Hornblower Series*. I thought that the greatest adventure a young man could have would be to go to sea. This ambition would later be fueled during my high school years by the *Victory at Sea* film series, a documentary on World War II naval warfare, which I was able to watch on Saturday afternoon television.

New Orleans Academy, or NOA as it was popularly known, required uniforms, so from 5th grade on, a uniform of some kind would be a way of life for me for the next forty-eight years. NOA was an all-boys school, and the owner and principal intentionally invited boys from all walks and stations of life to attend. When I graduated in June of 1957, NOA granted degrees to one of the largest classes in many years. Our class consisted of nineteen boys, three of which came from single parent homes. There was a good cross section of society.

I played on my first organized sports team beyond my Cub Scout football in 7th grade, and from then on sports became a very important part of my life. Because we were such a small school, I was able to play on teams in every sport. We did not have a baseball team, but we did have teams in football, basketball, and track. If I had attended a larger school, I probably would not have had such an opportunity. What I lacked in physical attributes, such as size, dexterity, speed, coordination, and strength, I was able to compensate for by sheer aggressiveness and determination. This worked well in football and track, but didn't work too well with the finesse sports such as basketball. I was able to break in as a starting defensive end on the football team as a sophomore, weighing in at less than 140 pounds. I was a kamikaze, willing to play defense with reckless abandon. I was also able to run the half mile and a leg of the mile relay team by my sophomore year. In basketball I had to settle for the junior varsity team until my senior year. I became a starter then, but only because we had just seven or eight guys on the team. In spite of that, we made it to Louisiana State quarter finals for our class of schools. We were blessed to have several outstanding athletes, two of which went on to Tulane University on athletic scholarships.

Summertime was a challenge for me and I felt at loose ends. The summer between fifth and sixth grades I tried to get steady employment, but no one would hire me even to bag groceries. I had to settle for sporadic yard work and odd jobs. My first real employment opportunity came after ninth grade when I was hired by one of my NOA teachers and coach who operated a day camp during the summer months. I became a counselor and swimming instructor, and this opportunity would remain available to me throughout my high school years.

Nicknames were commonplace at NOA, and mine was "Golden Boy", or "Goldie", as some would say. This was because some perceived that I always did what was right. Contrarily, my younger brother, Charlie, was always in trouble. Charlie was short in stature and determined to make up for what he lacked in height by being the toughest kid on the block. Many years later, I confided to Charlie that there was nothing he had done that I probably had not done myself, but Charlie always seemed to get caught. I really didn't mind my nickname, for it was used by some whom I considered close friends and I really didn't perceive its use as derision or ridicule.

I wish I could say that I lived up to or deserved the nickname, but in reality, I didn't. I did, however, have a sensitive conscience and no one knew the difficulty I had in dealing with guilt and remorse. New Orleans is predominately Catholic and many of my friends were of the Catholic faith. I envied them. They could go to confession every Saturday afternoon and then start over again on Saturday night with a clear conscience. I had to continue to deal with my guilt and try to rationalize my bad behavior. To this day I am amazed at my ability to convince myself that I'm not "that bad" and to rationalize or excuse unacceptable conduct. Back then I just had to continue to ensure that my good deeds outnumbered the bad.

As far as difficulties or hardships, I considered my life uneventful until my senior year of high school. I had worked at the day camp for most of the summer, spending a lot of the time teaching swimming and I consequently developed a sinus infection. In the meantime I had been selected to participate in Pelican Boys State, an event held for selected seniors at Louisiana State University in Baton Rouge. It was designed to introduce us to statewide policies and provide a time in which we would participate in mock campaigns and elections.

When I returned from Baton Rouge, I jumped right into football practice which had already begun. The fluid forming behind my eardrum from my sinus infection had begun to affect my hearing so I finally saw an Ear Nose and Throat specialist, just before the opening game of the season. The doctor told me that I had to stop playing football until the infection cleared. When I told the coach, he asked me not to tell the team. We were anticipating a very successful season and perhaps the possibility of having more wins than losses, something that had not happened at NOA in many years. He said, "Go ahead and dress out. I won't use you unless I really need you." However, he put me in the game immediately after the opening kickoff and I played the remainder of the game. We won that game, defeating the league's previous year's champions. On the trip home, I felt feverish and had difficulty hearing. My trip to the ENT the following week was unpleasant, to say the least. The doctor punctured my eardrums, drained my ears, and irrigated my sinuses by pushing a large needle through the rear wall of my nasal passages so that water could be pumped into the lower sinus cavity. It felt like I had a spike driven through my face. Then I saw water shoot out of my eye as the water pressure was applied. Very unpleasant, indeed.

The thing that concerned me most was that damage to my sinuses might affect my ability to be accepted to the Naval Academy. I decided that I would comply with the doctor's instruction. I fully expected that with the doctor's care, the problem would be cleared and I could resume football in a week or two. Each week I was asked by the coach and my teammates when I would return, and as the season progressed, it became apparent that the coach and team were more concerned with the success of the team than with my health or personal plans and ambitions. The message conveyed was, "you'd better watch out for yourself, because no one else will". This was certainly the hardest time that I had experienced in my short life and a lesson that would shape my life for the next sixteen years.

The football season finally came to an end and I accepted the fact that, even though others may not accept the reasons for my remaining on the sidelines, I would just have to steel myself against their perceptions and move on. I had surgery during Christmas vacation of that year and my doctor made permanent holes from the lower sinus cavity directly into the nasal passages, so that the lower sinus cavity could continually drain. As a result of this procedure, I would never, during my time as a fighter pilot and later on the airline, have to miss a flight because of a cold or sinus problem. Years later, when I conferred with my flight surgeon, he didn't believe me until he looked and saw the openings for himself.

I was able to begin basketball following Christmas break- but really, after the discouraging fall of my senior year, I was just waiting for high school to come to an end so I could move on.

My dad didn't have much political pull, so when congressional selection time came for the Naval Academy, I was awarded an alternate appointment. My congressman tried to get me to accept an appointment to the newly founded Air Force Academy or to the Coast Guard Academy. Neither one of these institutions appealed, for I wanted a commission in the Navy. I wanted one day to be an Admiral. After retirement from the Navy, I imagined that I might enter politics and one day even become President of the United States. I thought to myself, "Reach high; shoot for the stars and even if you fall short you may come up with the moon".

As a back-up or alternate plan, I applied and took the tests for a regular Navy ROTC scholarship. In the process of taking ACT tests, three of us in my NOA senior class were National Merit Honor finalists. We were three of twenty-something in the whole city.

I did receive a Navy ROTC scholarship and filled out applications for many universities with NROTC units, including Rice, Georgia Tech, several Ivy League universities, and Tulane. I was accepted for admittance to Tulane University as well as their Navy ROTC unit, so as high school graduation approached, I assumed I would be going to Tulane.

Following graduation, I opened my own swimming school and had started my first classes when an unexpected telegram arrived instructing me to report to the Naval Academy on July 1. My family planned to drive me to Annapolis as part of a family vacation. I had never been further north than North Carolina, so it was an interesting trip. We stopped in Washington D.C., where we spent several days enjoying the sights before continuing on to Annapolis.

# CHAPTER 2

The family dropped me off at about noon July 1 on the grounds of the Naval Academy, the Yard, with a small overnight bag. I immediately began processing in. When asked what kind of appointment I had received, I responded that I didn't know. I assumed that I had received a congressional appointment. It was only then that I found out I had received a Secretary of the Navy appointment, which had been awarded on a competitive basis.

Everything that I had brought with me was packed up and mailed home. Everything I now had was official Navy issue.

Those first few days were a whirlwind. I saluted everything that moved and finally one of the men in uniform informed me that I didn't need to salute him for he was simply a janitor and wasn't in the military service at all.

I initially had two roommates, one of whom was from the South. John Quarterman was from Brunswick, Georgia. He was an all-state fullback who had been recruited by Navy to play football. The other initial roommate, Dave Nelson, was assigned to a different company when the academic year began, and would decide to depart prior to the end of plebe year. John's high school classmate, Sandy Mock, was also at the Academy. We requested to room together, so when the academic year began, we were assigned to the same company and ended up rooming together for our entire four years. John would be instrumental in introducing me to my future bride. I would be his best man in his wedding in Pensacola, and he in turn would be best man in mine.

Roommates were assigned based on our selection of foreign language, two years of which were required. Since I had only studied Latin, I felt that if I had chosen a language such as Spanish, French, or German, I would probably end up in class with others who had already had some exposure to their selected language and therefore I would be behind before we even started. I didn't know anyone who had studied Brazilian Portuguese and, since I also heard that it was relatively simple, I chose Portuguese. In retrospect it would have been good to learn German. But then I would not have roomed with John and Sandy, who chose Portuguese for the same reasons I did. John, Sandy, and I have remained lifelong friends.

Plebe year was a challenge. That summer was a great adventure, but when the upperclassmen returned in the fall, I felt like I was just fighting to survive. Hazing was commonplace and the challenge of staying ahead of the upperclassmen's requisite questions preempted the allocated study time for classroom academics. I soon found that my high school preparation in math and science was sorely lacking. Every math class had a quiz and I had no background in the use of a slide rule. As a result, I was trying to work multiplications by hand and was always behind. Chemistry was a complete mystery. We had a shower in our room with an overhead light, and since lights had to be out at 10:30, I would get up at 3 or 4 am, hang a blanket over the shower curtain rod so the light could not be seen, and sit and study on the shower floor. I entered mid-year finals with a grade that was marginal, but my extra study paid off and I managed to get a math final grade that pulled me through. We had four years of math at the

Academy, and ironically, by senior year, math was my highest grade. At the end of plebe year, I was at about the fifty percent placement in my class, but by the time of graduation I was in the top twenty percent. Class standing is extremely important at the Naval Academy for that is what determines your order for service selection upon graduation. Since there is a quota for each branch of service, if your standing is not high enough, you may not be able to get your choice.

I've read that Robert E. Lee made it through West Point without a single demerit. Any aspirations I had of equaling such an accomplishment were shattered by Lt. "Blackjack" Scoville. I was standing watch that day as "mate of the deck". My duties were to oversee the security of the 13th company area of Bancroft Hall on one deck or floor. If a company officer or the Officer of the Day came on deck, I was to chop up to him, salute and render the appropriate salutation, which in this case was, "Good morning, Sir". I fulfilled my appropriate duties and "Blackjack" proceeded through the area without further word. Shortly after, I received word to report to the battalion office to sign a report. On reporting to the office, I found that I had been put on report for "disrespect". The report said that Midshipman Fourth Class Klumpp was on report for "disrespect" because he said, "Good morning, Suh". Obviously, Lt. Scoville was not a southern gentleman. Well, so much for demerit-free.

"Hundredth Night" was time for payback. It was one-hundred days before graduation and the night that plebes switched places with the first classmen. It was their opportunity to return the hazing they had received. Even though I knew I would pay a price and hundredth night was several weeks away, I selected two of the worst first classmen in our company and issued them a "come around". Days before the big revenge night, I came down with measles and spent my hundredth night quarantined in the Naval Academy Hospital.

In preparation for the summer months' cruise, large wooden boxes were distributed to each midshipman. These cruise boxes were to be the storage unit for all of our personal uniforms and equipment that we would not need while on cruise or other summer deployments. After graduation we would take our boxes with us or have them shipped to our first duty station. Mine has served me well over all these years and presently sits in my garage where it holds paint brushes, rags and other painting paraphernalia.

Little did we know that when our new cruise boxes arrived in the hall outside of our rooms that they would provide the source of one last sporting event for plebes- "Cruise box races". The upperclassmen would have the plebe report in one uniform and then change into a completely different uniform, all within the confines of the box while it was closed. The race was pitting one plebe against another and the loser was simply subjected to further harassment.

The only serious trouble that I had occurred right at the end of plebe year, or you might say, the beginning of youngster year. As June Week approached, we managed to acquire unauthorized civilian attire, which consisted of a pair of Bermuda shorts and a sport shirt. The purpose for the clothing was to shed the uniform while engaging for a short time in social activities with our June Week dates off the grounds of the Naval Academy. In this case, some of our classmates and I had pooled our resources to rent a house in Sherwood Forest where our dates could stay, properly chaperoned by a set of midshipman's parents. It was graduation day and, since following graduation our class had officially placed a plebe cap at the pinnacle of a properly greased Herndon

Monument, we were now appropriately considered youngsters or Midshipmen Third Class.

Following the ceremonies, we adjourned to Sherwood Forest where we celebrated our new status by engaging in the consumption of unauthorized cold canned adult beverages. When time came to return to the Academy, my roommate John and I shed our Bermuda shorts and donned our uniforms only to discover that someone had stolen our caps. A midshipman's cap was prized by other students who either didn't aspire or didn't have the privilege of attending such an institution. Thus, we had to return to Mother Bancroft sans caps.

Liberty was to expire shortly and as we approached the gate to the Academy, we knew that there would probably be an officer at the gate. He could certainly stop and question us concerning being out of uniform and in questioning, he would discover that we had participated in other unauthorized activities. We quickly decided that our best option was to go over the wall. John and I are the only midshipmen I know of who went over the wall during liberty hours to get back in. As we sprinted toward Mother Bancroft, we spotted the Officer of the Day at the top of the stairs to the main entrance and knew we had one more hurdle to negotiate before we were home safe. Spotting an open window on the main floor, we quickly determined that a reasonable leap across a basement level well would place us safely home. The only problem was, the shades were pulled and we had no way of knowing what we might find on the other side of the shades. You can only imagine the surprise of the two occupants as the shade flew back and two midshipmen rolled across their desk. To our good fortune we found the room to be occupied by other new third-class midshipmen. Our jubilation was short lived, however, for as we exited into the hallway, we were met by a brand new First Classman relishing his new status at having finally scaled to the top.

The remainder of our evening was spent mourning the fact that our entire summer on Youngster Cruise would be spent restricted to the ship, which would have been more than one might endure. A friend and new First Classman from New Orleans, Pete Bevins, was in a different battalion and just happened to stop by. After I had sadly related our predicament, he said that he would see what he could do. Pete returned early the next morning and informed us that all charges had been dropped. What I failed to mention is that Pete was Brigade Boxing Champion and I highly suspect that, considering the attitude of the First Classman who had put us on report, Pete probably threatened to punch his lights out. We were not restricted and that summer I had the delightful pleasure of visiting Oporto, Portugal; Copenhagen, Denmark, and Antwerp, Belgium. Between ports, I chipped paint and stood boiler room watches on the *Vogelgesang*, a World War II vintage destroyer.

Third class year was, for the most part, unremarkable. I seemed to have caught up with the pack and held my own in math and the sciences. My big adventure was joining the Ocean Sailing Team. Plebe year I had participated in a number of intramural athletic endeavors, but I found that ocean sailing allowed one to get away from the confines of the Yard on weekends and cruise the Chesapeake Bay. Another enticement was that they usually boarded a stash of rum, for medicinal purposes only, of course.

At the end of my second year, our class was to proceed to Little Creek, Virginia, for several weeks of amphibious training. Since the *Highland Light*, our seventy-foot sloop, was to participate in the Annapolis to New Port, Rhode Island Ocean Race, we were able to remain in Annapolis. So, when our class embarked to Little Creek, Sandy Mock, Ed Keller, and I caught the train to New Your City. What followed were three days of the Latin Quarter, Rockefeller Center, and Greenwich Village. We then returned to make final preparations for the ocean race.

The remainder of the summer included time with the aviation units in Jacksonville and Pensacola, Florida. The most significant event was meeting Ann Cassell. Ann was Sandy's date for a party at John's sister's home in Brunswick, where we had gone on one of our weekends in Jacksonville. Ann was a beautiful little thing with a charming soft southern accent and nice quiet calm manner.

Christmas break in each of my years at the Academy was very eventful. The New Orleans Debutante Season had already begun by the time I arrived home, and Naval Academy midshipmen and West Point cadets were considered worthwhile prospects. A high school friend, Charlie Green, was in the same class at West Point, and we took full advantage of the New Orleans social scene. One year I had two weeks leave and twenty-three invitations.

Second class year, which was considered the most challenging year academically, moved rather quickly. I had established a pattern at the Academy. When I worked, I worked hard, and when I played, I played with the same intensity. I left the Varsity sailing team and went back to intramural sports, and my biggest challenge came in the spring as head of the company knockabout team. The knockabouts were beautiful little day-sailing sloops. The Naval Academy had a nice fleet of them which were used for training, recreation, and intramural competition.

My big day came on a choppy, windy afternoon in the Chesapeake Bay when I managed to wipe out three knockabouts. Racing a triangular course, I managed to remove the masts on two of the other competitors' boats, one as we were rounding the first buoy and another at the second buoy. Even though they knew

I had the right of way according to the rules of the road, both of the boats tried to bluff me. They were commanded by First-Class Midshipmen who knew I was only a Second-Classman. I was not going to give way to a bluff, however, even from an upperclassman. Aggression works well in some sports, but I don't recommend it too strongly in sailing. We finished the race and returned our boat to its slip. The other two boats had to be towed in.

What ensued was quite harrowing and I spent many hours studying the Rules of the Road and preparing my defense. The head of the small craft facility on the opposite bank of the Severn wanted me to spend every free minute for the remainder of the year working at his facility. I had my hearing before several company officers. I felt as if I were facing a court martial, but when the dust settled, I was exonerated. I have no idea of what happened to the First-Class Midshipmen who had commanded the other boats. This incident did, however, end my Naval Academy sailing career, for I had no desire to push my luck.

First class summer included another cruise and this time I visited the Mediterranean aboard the *Forrestal*. My only time in port consisted of two weeks in Cannes France. I did have a brief stopover in Spain on the way over and Port Leaute, French Morocco, on the way back. The most significant event of my summer was another visit to Brunswick, Georgia. This time Ann Cassell was my date. She was a blind date and although I remembered who she was, I had made such an impression on her the previous summer that she hadn't a clue who I was. The only reason she accepted was that she had nothing better to do. She initially declined to accept the date because she could only imagine what someone with a name like Fritz Klumpp could possibly look like. I ended up dating her each day of my five-day visit and began to write her upon my return to the Naval Academy.

The next opportunity to return to Brunswick arrived during Christmas leave. Charlie Lyman, a classmate from New Iberia, Louisiana, was driving his car back to the Academy, so I planned to ride back with him. After a few days in New Orleans, we proceeded to Brunswick, which was to be a stopover on our way to Miami where Navy was scheduled to play Missouri in the Orange Bowl. We never made it past Brunswick, however, and remained there for the rest of our leave. I dated Ann once again. She was my choice, but for Ann, our New Year's Eve date came about simply because her first choice never called.

The Brigade of Midshipmen was scheduled to participate in the Inaugural Parade for newly elected president, Senator John Fitzgerald Kennedy. It was an unforgettable experience, not because of the event itself but because of the weather. Washington was covered with snow and temperatures were sub-freezing. Competition in everything between academics and sports determines each year who the color company will be. The winner is awarded special privileges including attending extra football games and selecting the June Week Color Girl. The Thirteenth Company had been the Color Company the year before and as such we were to bear the colors or flags for the Brigade of Midshipmen. My role in the color guard was that of carrying a rifle, and my position was on the left side closest to the reviewing stand. The uniform of the day included overcoats and rubber galoshes. Marching with rubber galoshes was not so bad until someone stepped on the heel of the person ahead. This resulted in the rear of the galoshes breaking free of the heel of the shoe, producing a flapping sound commonly referred to as a blowout. The only way to silence the flapping sound was to kick galoshes free of the entire shoe. The Brigade of Midshipmen made their memorable mark on the inaugural event by leaving rubber galoshes strewn all the way down Pennsylvania Avenue.

We were all invited to attend inaugural events celebrating the Presidential Inauguration, but we were so cold that by the end of the parade all I could think about was returning to Bancroft Hall and a hot shower.

The second half of our first-class year was selection time. By now I had progressed far enough up the ladder in class standing to be pretty much assured of getting my first choice. In fact, academically I had made the Superintendent's List for the first time.

I had decided over my four years that either nuclear power submarines or aviation was a little more elitist and might offer opportunity for more rapid advancement. At the time, Admiral Rickover was interviewing each candidate for the nuclear power program and I was scheduled for an interview. However, when it was my turn to travel to Washington D.C. for the interview, I was having minor corrective surgery at the Naval Academy Hospital and didn't get the word. When I found that I had missed my interview, I simply shrugged it off and determined that the hand of fate had destined that I was to go into naval aviation instead.

I invited Ann to be my date for June Week and June Week of First-Class year finally arrived. Ann's parents, James and Marguerite, as well as my parents and youngest brother, Mike, were all present for the festivities.

# CHAPTER 3

On Graduation Day President John F. Kennedy gave the commencement address. We received our diplomas and commissions, tossed our caps into the air, and had our mothers and dates pin on our new shoulder boards. I had it made.

The next day we loaded up our new automobiles and departed Mother Bancroft for the last time. My mother had promised me when I was in high school that if I won a scholarship to college, she would insure that when I graduated, I would receive a new automobile. Determined not to take advantage of my parents' generosity I wanted to choose a car that would be practical, not extravagant. I determined that either a Volkswagen beetle or a small Swedish Volvo would fit the bill and of these two the Volvo was far and above the better choice. That Volvo PV-544, termed "the family sports car", was probably the best car I have ever owned. It could easily reach a highway speed of ninety-five mph, got better than twenty-five miles per gallon, and never burned a drop of oil.

I had the privilege of driving Ann home to Brunswick. For me this drive was the culmination of a process that had begun with our first date. On that very first date, after she was safely inside the screen door, I had said, "I love you, Ann Cassell". I was as surprised as she was at my words. It was not like me to say something so impulsive, but I was just expressing what I felt. Her thoughts expressed later were, "What a line!"

By the time we arrived in Brunswick, I was hooked. I had thirty days leave before I had to report to Pensacola. I spent much of that time thinking about my next step. I determined that Ann was the woman I wanted to spend the rest of my life with. If I didn't grab her, someone else would. I expected to be moving very fast career-wise, so I had better seize the opportunity while I had a chance.

Ann visited New Orleans, and on my twenty-second birthday, July 2, my parents had a party for me in their home. Ann and I took a break from the festivities, and during that break I asked Ann if she would marry me. To my surprise, she said yes.

Ann returned to Brunswick and I reported to Pensacola. We had not talked specifically about a wedding date, but assumed our wedding would take place in about a year. After two weeks in Pensacola, I called Ann and asked if we could move the date up to Christmas. Ann said yes.

Approximately a week passed before I called again to see if we could move the date up again, this time to Thanksgiving. Ann once again replied yes.

A week later I called and asked Ann how soon she could get to Pensacola. We set a date for Friday, September 29. Since Pensacola was about midway between Brunswick and New Orleans, it would be equally accessible by both our families and friends. I would make the arrangements with the Air Station, so I spoke to the Chaplain and we scheduled the wedding at the base chapel for 6:00 Friday evening, with a reception to follow at the Officers' Club.

After the arrangements were completed and I had invited four of my classmates to serve as best man and ushers, we received a briefing from the Safety Officer. We were just about to complete the preflight part of our training and the safety briefing was in anticipation of the commencement of actual flying.

Shortly after the beginning of his presentation, the Safety

Officer said, "Whatever you do, don't try to get married while you are going through flight training. If you do, you will never make it". I looked around the room and all eyes were on me. I figured that it was too late to do anything else at this point. Perhaps if I had known the toll that the pressures would take on our relationship as newlyweds, I would have bitten the bullet and postponed our plans until after I had received my wings.

Prior to the wedding, I gave Ann a copy of a Navy classic, *The Navy Wife*. I also told her that the Navy would always have to come first. It is difficult for me now to imagine someone accepting such terms without question, but she did and our wedding took place as scheduled. The Navy gave me Friday afternoon off and Ann and I had the weekend to honeymoon in Fort Walton before I had to be back to work on Monday morning. I had just completed my fifth flight in the T-34 *Mentor* by the time of the wedding.

Since childhood, I've had a history of motion sickness and this was initially a concern. Every time I flew, I felt queasy and, though I never did, I felt like I might throw up. However, once I took the controls of the aircraft, the feeling would subside.

There are several milestones in flying, the first of which is your first solo flight. I'll never forget the day that my instructor told me to make a full stop landing at one of the outlying grass fields. He then exited the aircraft, instructing me to take off, fly once around the pattern and land. I proceeded to take off and as I climbed out, I remember looking back and thinking, "Well, you've done it now. You have no choice but to land this thing."

A big breakthrough in my training came in the next phase of our primary flight training: aerobatics. It was then, when I was flying solo and began doing aileron rolls, barrel rolls, loops, Immelmanns, and spins, that I fell in love with flying. It was totally exhilarating and I experienced a sense of freedom unlike anything I had ever known.

When I first arrived at Pensacola, it was my intent to pursue a flying career that would take me into anti-submarine warfare. My reasoning was that there was a lag in our ability to detect enemy submarines, and if I were engaged in anti-submarine warfare when the breakthrough in sub detection came, I might be able to ride the crest of the wave to early promotion. When the time came for selection for the next phase of training however, all of my classmates who had aspired to fly favored a selection of jets which would lead to attack or fighters. "Besides," they said, "the jets are air conditioned and not as hot as props." That settled it. My grades were high enough, so jets it would be.

Before we even departed Pensacola for Meridian, Mississippi and Basic Training in the T-2 *Buckeye*, Ann realized that she was gaining weight and I quickly deducted that she was pregnant.

So now, not only was I a newlywed trying to maneuver my way through the mine field of flight training, but I was also going to have the responsibility of fatherhood. Don't misunderstand. I would have it no other way now, especially when I consider the beautiful baby girl and precious daughter that arrived the following June. But it did take a period of adjustment for me and the sense of responsibility was heavy.

Our time in Meridian continued to be a one of adjustment with many challenges. Training-wise, we were introduced to instrument and formation flying. For me, flying in close formation with other aircraft was the highlight. I believe that the coordinated flying of high-performance jet aircraft in close proximity is the ultimate team sport. At the completion of basic training in Meridian, we returned to Pensacola for gunnery and carrier landing qualification.

The only failed flight that I experienced in my training was the first time I was scheduled to fly aboard a carrier. We had started the day very early with field landing practice- simulated carrier approaches on a land-based runway. After our final practice, we were to stand by in the ready room until we received a "Charlie Time", Navy jargon for overhead and landing time at the ship. Charlie Time finally came at 1500 and I got all the way to the ship before experiencing radio failure. I returned to base and joined the next flight to the carrier. By the time I finally got into the traffic pattern at the ship, I was physically drained. I managed to get one touch and go landing but only after two wave-offs. The Landing Signal Officer, or Paddles, as he is called (a carry-over from the early days when the LSO gave help to the pilots with the use of paddles), said "Get that man out of my pattern". By that time, I was just sightseeing.

When I arrived back at base, I was devastated. All of my

buddies were going to Happy Hour to celebrate their carrier qualification and all I could do was think, "I'm supposed to be a Navy pilot and I can't even land on a ship." I went home and collapsed until the next morning when I was scheduled for two additional periods of Field Carrier Landing Practice. After those periods, the LSO said he couldn't see why I would have any trouble, so the next Monday I was scheduled to try the ship again. This time my carrier landings went as planned and after several touch and go landings, I experienced my first arrested landings and catapult shots. Taking a cat shot from aircraft carrier is both figuratively as well as literally a real kick. Now that Basic Training was complete, we packed our little Volvo and headed for Advanced Flight Training in Kingsville, Texas.

The night before ground school final exams, I finished my studies and went to bed rather early. I wanted to be sure that I was well rested. Ann soon awakened me asking if I would rub her back as she was experiencing back pains. Neither of us realized that she was in labor. A short time later, she awakened me again and I rubbed her back once more. The third time she awakened me, I asked her to get her bag because I was going to take her to the hospital. When we arrived at the hospital a nurse immediately put her in a wheel chair and took her up the elevator to delivery. At that time, husbands were not allowed to accompany their wives to delivery. I asked the nurse at the desk what I should do. She responded that I might as well go home as it could be quite some time until she delivered. I gave her my telephone number, instructed her to call me if anything happened, and went home and went back to bed. Upon awakening in the morning, I called the hospital to check on her progress and when I was informed that it could still be quite some time, I proceeded to the base and took my finals. Finishing, I called the hospital once more and when I was told that she was about to deliver, I went directly to the hospital, arriving just in time to see our beautiful new baby daughter, Denise. I thought I had done so well in handling this father business. Once again, I didn't have a clue. My impending responsibilities as a father had impressed me to work harder than I ever had before, and as a result of those finals I was selected Student of the Year. I had never finished at the head of my class in anything. Little did I know that I had added salt to Ann's wounds.

In advanced training, we started our flying in the F-9F *Cougar* jet and finished up in the F-11 Grumman *Tiger.* I loved the flying in Kingsville.

Once we completed our advanced Instrument Training in the F-9, the rest of the flying was great. We did our carrier landing qualifications again, this time in the F-9 and then we moved on to the Grumman *Tiger.* Since all of the F-11 aircraft had a single seat, our first flight in the F-11 would be solo. The F-11, which was being flown by the Navy Flight Demonstration Team, the Blue Angels, was capable of going transonic.

During our first flight in the F-11 we were to climb to altitude, go to full power, and put the aircraft in a thirty-degree dive. We could then for the first-time experience flying faster than the speed of sound. As I accelerated through Mach one my engine oil pressure gage dropped to zero. The procedure for loss of oil pressure required that the power be set to approximately seventy percent and remain at that position until you were on the ground. The engine could then be expected to run anywhere from thirty seconds to thirty minutes. I notified base and proceeded to a high key position over the field. From that position I could conceivably spiral down in an engine out approach. Of course, they never would have allowed me as a student to attempt an engine out landing. If the engine had failed completely, they would have ordered me to eject. It seemed as if everyone and his brother was trying to give me instructions and I remember just wishing that they would shut up and let me concentrate on flying the aircraft. I inched the power up just a bit on short final and safely landed. I especially enjoyed the fighter tactics and dog fighting in the F-11.

We trained together in flights of three students and one instructor, and when it came time to receive our Navy Wings of Gold in November 1962, we thought we were the luckiest guys alive. Our flight, consisting of Bill Wilson, Phil Butler and me, was the first flight to receive fleet orders in over a year. The other students had been sent to Glynco NAS in Brunswick, Georgia, to fly as targets for radar training, or to Maintenance School in Memphis, or to plow back as flight instructors in Pensacola. Bill Wilson received orders to an F-8 *Crusader* Photo Recon Squadron at Miramar, California, Phil Butler received orders to an A-4 *Skyhawk* Light Attack Squadron at Lemoore, California, and I received orders to VF-114, an F-4 *Phantom* Squadron at Miramar. VF-114 was the first F-4 Squadron on the West Coast, and the *Phantom* was, at that time, considered the world's hottest fighter. Bill Wilson subsequently would be shot down and rescued three times over North Vietnam. Phil Butler, after having his bombs detonate prematurely due to faulty fusing, would be captured and held as a prisoner of war in Hanoi for seven and a half years.

# CHAPTER 4

A rriving at NAS Miramar in San Diego, we settled our young family, Ann, Denise and me, in a rental house in Poway. The subdivision was having a dispute with the developer and many of the homes had been vacated by the new owners. We were given an opportunity to buy our three-bedroom, two bath home for $19,000. All we had to do was to take over payments of $99.50 a month, which is what we were paying in rent. "What would we want with a home in California?" I thought. "I don't want to be a landlord." Oh, if only we had known.

I reported to the Replacement Air Group Squadron, or RAG, as it is commonly known, and began my training in the F-4 Phantom.

My classmate from the Naval Academy, Terry Murphy, reported at the same time. Terry had completed his training in Beeville, Texas, at the same time I had finished at Kingsville. Terry and his wife, Claire, and Ann and I were to become good friends as we went through our training in the RAG.

"You'd better pull the gear up quickly," said Terry. Terry had just completed his first flight as I was preparing for mine. The aircraft accelerated so fast he said that if you didn't get the gear up quickly, you would exceed the landing gear speed limitations. There I was, flying the world's fastest fighter! What a thrill!

I have a framed photograph on the wall of my study of a light aircraft stuck in a tree. The large print above the photo says: "Aviation in itself is not inherently dangerous. But to an even greater degree than the sea, it is terribly unforgiving of any carelessness, incapacity or neglect."

Early during my training in the F-4 Replacement Air Group Squadron (RAG), I was scheduled for a round-robin night familiarization flight. Since we were scheduled to take off and land back at Miramar NAS, I decided that my approach plates for Miramar would be all that I would need to safely return to base. All of the RAG Radar Intercept Officers that I had flown with had always carried a full navigation package with approach plates for all of the airfields in the area, so if by any chance I should need more, my RIO would have the approach plates I might require for an alternate field.

Our flight went as planned until we began our instrument penetration and approach back into Miramar. At about twenty miles from the runway, approach control asked "How is the visibility?"

"Clear", I responded, "I can see the runway." At about ten miles out they asked again to which I responded the same. They asked once more as I passed the five-mile point. Suddenly at two miles the runway and approach lights completely disappeared. Approach control reported ceiling and visibility zero. Welcome to San Diego. I rapidly learned about sea fog rolling in from the ocean. As I pushed my throttles forward and began executing the missed approach procedure, I asked my RIO to give me navigation information for Yuma MCAS. "Don't you have your charts and approach plates? I didn't bring any with me."

So, there we were, heading east with no idea where we were going or how we would get there. "Now I've done it. Here I am with the world's greatest fighter and I am going to end up landing it out in the middle of the desert". After long anxious minutes, we were able to contact a radar site and get a steer to a small auxiliary field at El Centro, California. We landed uneventfully, I contacted the squadron at Miramar, and we spent the night. Some things pilots just don't talk about and this is perhaps the first time I've told anyone of this incident.

The Navy's first F-4s were intended to be all-weather interceptors and they were not configured for air to ground weapons delivery. However, they were designed to intercept incoming enemy aircraft at high altitudes which included altitudes above fifty thousand feet. In order to fly above fifty thousand feet pilots are required to wear full pressure suits, so I was fitted with a full pressure suit similar to what our astronauts wear. I did enjoy my first high altitude attempt in which I was able to reach well over seventy thousand feet. You're really just at the peak of a trajectory at that point and along for the ride. The air is so thin the aircraft flight controls are ineffective. The only problem with the pressure suit is that every time I would wear it when flying I felt totally indestructible. I felt like I could fly right through a brick wall. I knew enough at this point to realize that a feeling of indestructibility was not conducive to flying safely.

There are several unforgettable experiences in becoming a Naval Aviator. Two of these I have already mentioned: an aviator's first solo flight and first catapult shot and arrested landing. The third and last one was to occur near the conclusion of our training in the RAG: night carrier landings.

In preparation for night carrier qualifications, we practiced field carrier landing for what seemed an eternity. One of the runways at Miramar and a runway on San Clemente Island just off the coast of California were configured with lighting simulating the deck lighting of a carrier. That is where we did most of our carrier landing practice.

Our day for carrier qualifications finally arrived and Terry and I boarded the *Kittyhawk* and were soon sitting in the ready room waiting for our turn. After we completed our day qualifications, we again waited. This time it was for our night quals. When it was my turn, I manned the aircraft, which was parked on the forward elevator at the hangar deck level. As I sat strapped in, anxiously waiting for them to raise the elevator to the flight deck, I saw salt spray blowing against the windscreen, and as I looked out into the dark night, I couldn't help but wonder just what I had gotten myself into. Little did I know.

When they finally did bring me to the flight deck, I went

into automatic mode. Before I even knew it, I had finished three night cat shots and three night traps. For those first three, I was in a state of shock, and it wasn't until my fourth landing that I finally came out of automatic. On the fourth trap, I blew a tire, so that finished me for the night. Since we needed six traps to be qualified, I had to stay aboard and complete the remaining two on the next and final night aboard.

Following carrier qualifications, I was ready to report to VF-114, which had just returned from their first West Pac (Western Pacific) deployment with the F-4. Since it was the first F-4 squadron on the West Coast, it was comprised of a very select group of seasoned pilots, and three of us, Bill Blunt, Joe Skubi and I were the first replacements.

"Blunt, Klumpp, and Skubi reporting for duty."

"What are we getting here, a vaudeville act?" quipped the Duty Officer.

"What is it like being in a fighter squadron?" someone asked. The unknown respondent answered, "It's like belonging to a motorcycle gang and still having your mother be proud of you."

My tour with the Aardvarks was truly one of my life's greatest experiences. Our initial mission was to be an all-weather interceptor, protecting the fleet from enemy attack. Because the profile of the F-4 aircraft was similar to that of another interceptor, the BC comic strip aardvark ZOT, VF114 had adopted the nickname "Aardvarks".

The first big event after my arrival was a firepower demonstration for the then president, John F. Kennedy. A rocking chair was placed on the flight deck for the president. For our part of the air power demonstration, VF-114 had four aircraft flying in formation, line abreast, that were to simultaneously fire four Sparrow missiles head-on against an F-9F *Cougar* as the target aircraft. As a newcomer, I didn't get to fly in the event, but it was exciting nonetheless to be a part of an historic event.

In October 1963, we were scheduled to deploy to Westpac for what was supposed to be a six-month cruise. In preparation for this deployment, we put our household goods in storage and Ann and Denise boarded a flight for Brunswick. We had planned for them to spend the time of our deployment with Ann's parents. Not a good decision. It was very hard on Ann, for it is not easy to live in a parent's home once one has moved out, become independent, and established their own home. As it turned out, that six-month cruise would be extended to nine months.

On the way to the western Pacific, I experienced another of those unforgettable milestones in the life of a Navy pilot. We were in the middle of the Pacific Ocean, well out of range of any divert fields. I was scheduled for a night launch. It was one of those dark nights that many pilots find unforgettable even when everything goes as planned. It doesn't get much darker than a night at sea, without a moon and without the glow of lights from a nearby city or town. During my first cruise, we still operated under the rules that were a carryover from World War II, when ships were darkened so the enemy could not visually detect their position. Because of this, the deck lighting was minimal, even during recovery.

As I proceeded down the track on my catapult shot, my airspeed indicator stopped at eighty knots and my altimeter began to unwind-indicating below sealevel. Because of the G forces, I knew I had a good cat-shot, but I had no airspeed indicator or altimeter. I did have an attitude indicator, however, so I pulled the nose of the aircraft up and lit the afterburners. I must have been 20,000 feet before I could lower the nose. I joined up on the other squadron aircraft and simply flew formation on his wing until time for recovery.

My wingman was one of our seasoned pilots, so he brought me back into the landing pattern and stayed with me until I was lined up aft of the ship. On the first pass, I boltered or missed all of the arresting wires. On any carrier landing, the pilot is trained not to flare the aircraft or to break the rate of descent before touchdown, but to keep flying until he hits the deck. Flaring the aircraft on touchdown increases the risk of failing to engage a wire. He is also trained to go to full power and rotate for takeoff as soon as he hits the deck. This is in case he misses the arresting wires. He doesn't pull the power back until he is at a full stop and receives a signal to do so from the deck crew.

Following my bolter, my flight leader picked me up again and took me around the pattern for another pass. On the second pass, I got a wave-off from the LSO. There were no verbal communications, but he waved me off by the use of the red wave-off lights on the landing signal datum lights. The lights consist of a horizontal row of green datum lights crossed by a vertical row of white lights. The vertical lights only illuminate one light at a time and the illuminated light is called the meatball. These vertical lights provide the pilot with visual glideslope information and the objective for the pilot is to keep the meatball aligned with the green datum lights. As long as he keeps the meatball centered, he is on the proper glide path for a successful landing. By the third pass, things got worse and once again I received a wave-off.

Downwind, I began to wonder how cold the water was, for I only had fuel enough for one more pass before I would have to refuel from an airborne tanker. Fighters are the most fuel critical of carrier aircraft, and for this reason, the fighters are always brought aboard first. As I was turning final, the LSO communicated for the first time, "Okay, I've got my radios back now, so settle down". Oh, the calming effect of that steady voice. I couldn't understand why he had not said anything before. He had not said anything up until this point because he didn't have functioning radios. I got aboard on the fourth pass.

When I got to the ready room, I was expecting to be chewed out by the skipper Joe "Big Julie" Konzen. To my relief, Joe didn't say a thing. The seasoned RIOs, Radar Intercept Officers, who were the rear seat part of the F-4 team, said that they would have ejected on the cat shot. They had a rule: if they didn't have flight speed as indicated by the airspeed indicator, they were out of there. My RIO, Mike Murphy, was just as green as I was. Mike flew with me that entire cruise, but by the end of the cruise, Mike had had enough and turned in his wings.

During this cruise, we were at the height of the cold war and early one morning, shortly after we had arrived in the western Pacific, the captain of the ship came onto the ship's PA system and solemnly stated, "I have a very grave announcement."

"Oh, boy," I thought, "we have gone to war with Russia."

"The President, President John F. Kennedy, has just been assassinated." Another milestone.

Life can be such a dichotomy. I loved operating off a carrier. The flying was great and nothing in aviation can compare with taking a catapult shot off a carrier, hassling or dogfighting with other fighters, and landing back aboard the ship, especially on a clear, calm day. By the same token, nothing can be as challenging as landing on a pitching carrier deck on a dark night in a stormy sea. As much as I enjoyed the flying and what I was doing operationally, I found myself counting the days until I would be reunited with my precious wife and daughter. We visited exotic places: Sasebo, Kobe, and Yokosuka, Japan, and Hong Kong, but I especially missed not being able to share the sights and sounds with the one I held most dear.

Before our six months were completed, we were deployed to the Tonkin Gulf and ended up stationed at a remote place, defined only by coordinates, called Yankee Station. During this extended time, the F-4 aircraft flew CAP, or Combat Air Patrol missions to protect the fleet. Some of the photo recon aircraft flew missions into Laos. On one of these missions, LT Chuck Klusman was shot down and some of the F-8 *Crusaders* flew res-cap missions to try to recover him. We didn't know much about what was happening on the ground, but it seemed that the whole theater was heating up.

Finally, we were relieved and began our sail home. On arrival in San Diego, I immediately off-loaded my gear and, after picking up my car from my friend, Terry Murphy, in San Diego, drove non-stop to New Orleans. I was going to rest in New Orleans and then drive on to Brunswick, but Ann surprised me and had flown to New Orleans to meet me. We then drove to Brunswick where, after a visit with Ann's folks, we started back to San Diego.

On our way, we took the time to see some of the sights and worked at getting to know each other again. Such lengthy separations always require adjustments. I did consider myself extremely fortunate to have a wife that was such a great mother and always worked so hard to please her husband.

# CHAPTER 5

Shortly after our arrival back in San Diego, the Tonkin Gulf Incident occurred and we knew that during the next cruise, we would be experiencing full combat. Ann wanted another child, but I was fearful that if we had another and I was lost in combat, additional children would lessen her chance of remarrying and beginning a new life. Ann's desire prevailed, and in June 1965, our precious daughter, Karen, was born. I hardly got to know her before it was time to depart once again.

During our time between cruises, we received all new F-4s and our role was expanded from air-to-air combat with enemy aircraft, utilizing Sparrow and Sidewinder missiles, to include air-to-ground delivery of rockets and bombs.

Death had become an everyday occurrence in carrier aviation. I had lost several classmates through carrier mishaps during normal operations. My friend, Phil Butler, had to eject and was captured, and another friend, Jim Connell, had been shot down and captured as well. Phil was to spend those seven and a half years as a POW and Jim was tortured to death after five years of captivity.

We were taking care of Terry Murphy's automobile since his wife, Claire, had flown home with her daughter, Helen, to stay with her parents in New York, just as Ann and Denise had done during my first cruise. Claire was pregnant with their second child when Terry departed, and while he was deployed, she gave birth to their second daughter. Their new baby died of Sudden Infant Death Syndrome before Terry's scheduled return. Terry flew home to attend the funeral of the daughter whom he had never had the chance to see or hold, and then returned to join his squadron on the *Ranger* in the Tonkin Gulf.

As Claire was traveling back to San Diego to join Terry on his return, she received the news that he had been reported missing in action. Terry had been lost in an aerial engagement with MiGS. The Navy did not know how to reach Claire, so the first she knew of his being declared MIA was through the news media. Claire moved back to the east coast and we lost contact with her for the next fifteen years.

We departed San Diego and entered combat on Dixie Station the day after Thanksgiving, 1965. We flew close air support missions over South Vietnam for about five days before proceeding to Yankee Station and beginning our missions over the North.

Our Squadron Commander, Carl Austin, had scheduled himself to fly the first mission over North Vietnam. His RIO was LTJG Jake Logan. Our primary missions over the North were armed reconnaissance, part of the Rolling Thunder Operation, a limited interdiction strategy improvised by President Lyndon Johnson and Secretary of Defense, Robert McNamara.

Robert McNamara surrounded himself with his intellectual whiz kids and assumed that he knew much more than the professional military. He disregarded the recommendations of the Joint Chiefs and kept President Johnson from even knowing what they thought about how the war should be conducted. Johnson was more concerned with getting reelected so he could institute his "Great Society" domestic agenda and build his legacy. For this reason, he left everything concerning the conduct of the war to McNamara. McNamara's overall strategy was to slowly apply increasing pressure, believing that this would eventually lead North Vietnam to abandon their efforts to take over South Vietnam and bring it under communism. Meanwhile, the Joint Chiefs failed by allowing this to happen without effective opposition. I have said that it is a shame that there was not a military leader who would stand on principle regardless of the impact on his personal career. If he had, the American people would have at least gained an understanding of McNamara's failed policies and what was really going on in Vietnam.

Each mission was assigned a designated target, most of which were of limited strategic value. We were to fly to that target, looking for other unexpected opportunities to bomb along the way. Authorized targets of opportunity were limited to lines of communication and transportation. We seldom found anything moving, so the only thing that we could do to diminish transportation was to crater a road or bomb a bridge. In addition to the armed reconnaissance missions, we flew Barrier Combat Air Patrol or bar cap, photo escort, and an occasional Alpha Strike. The Alpha Strikes were the only missions with a meaningful target.

Several MiG's had been shot down by F-4's shortly after the bombing had begun. The MiG pilots had been surprised by the Sparrow Missile's head-on capability and would not engage. A fighter pilot is a gunslinger at heart and every fighter pilot is eager for an air to air combat kill. We would fly around and try to think of ways to entice them to come out and engage. It was only later that the MiGs would begin to get active. The purpose of our photo escort missions was again to provide fighter escort for the photo recon aircraft, and in the event that it was shot down by anti-aircraft fire, provide cover and report where the aircraft and pilot had gone down.

I was assigned squadron primary flight observer duty for the recovery of that first mission over the North. The pri-fly observer's role was to stand on the primary flight observation bridge on the ship's island and observe the return and recovery of the squadron's aircraft. I waited anxiously for the skipper's aircraft. It never returned. The reality of combat solemnly sank home.

My first combat mission over the North was at night. As an armed reconnaissance flight, we were assigned a stretch of highway and our objective was to try to detect and bomb any movement of vehicles. We were a flight of two F-4s and were given an armament load of four parachute flares and four 250 lb. banded lug bombs. Secretary of Defense McNamara had made a public statement that there was no bomb shortage, so here we were, risking two multimillion-dollar aircraft and the lives of four airmen with a total bomb load of 1000 lbs. The F-4, with its missile armament of 2 Sidewinders and 4 Sparrow missiles was capable of carrying 4000 lbs. of bombs. On this and many subsequent missions, we were carrying one-eighth of our capable load of ordnance. To add insult to injury, the 250 lb. bomb we were carrying, the ANM-57, was a Korean vintage bomb that had a banded lug added so that it could be adapted to the modern bomb racks. I recall watching one of these bombs hit the ground and not even detonate. The casing split open and it just smoked.

Since I was leading the flight, I was carrying the flares. I had briefed my wingman that if we spotted truck lights, I would roll in and illuminate the target with my flares, and he would then bomb. I spotted some lights which I assumed to be trucks. As I circled the target, I couldn't understand why the North Vietnamese weren't turning off their lights, for surely they could hear the F-4s. They were doing the opposite and turning on more and more lights. It suddenly dawned on me; those aren't truck lights, those are the muzzle flashes of North Vietnamese anti-aircraft guns!

I had flown three night missions over North Vietnam before I even got to see what it looked like in the daytime. We soon determined that it was better not to use the parachute flares at all, for the flares simply alerted the gunners, so they were armed and ready knowing that another aircraft would soon follow. We decided that it would be much more productive to create a sonic boom and drop the flares over a city on the way back to the ship as a means of harassing the enemy.

December was the height of the monsoon season, and many nights it was futile to even try to find a target. Nonetheless, we continued to launch, for the Navy was in competition with the Air Force to see who would record the greatest number of sorties. For the first time I realized that there were some senior military officers who didn't care how many dead bodies they had to step across to ensure their next promotion. I was now one of the seasoned veterans, so I was scheduled when the weather was worst. If you had successfully gotten back aboard once under these conditions, they knew that you could handle the stormy dark nights, so you were scheduled over and over again.

The events of Dec. 17, 1965, are indelibly imprinted in my mind. I launched as number two in a section of F-4s that were scheduled for a Rolling Thunder mission over North Vietnam. The flight leader was Lt. Felix Templeton. We each carried a bomb load of four ANM-57 bombs. In addition to the bombs, we carried our air-to-air armament of two Sidewinders and four Sparrow missiles. Because of the weather reports, we briefed to descend to 2000 feet over the water. Since we had no terrain clearance radar, if we did not break out of the overcast by 2000 feet, we would not cross the coast, for flying across unknown terrain below 2000 feet without terrain radar was pure stupidity.

We launched at 0110 going into the clouds and instrument flight conditions right off the catapult. We were to remain in instrument flight conditions or "in the soup" for the entire flight. Unable to descend below the clouds to find a target, we dumped our bombs on Tiger Island utilizing radar mapping to try to locate the island. For those of my generation, it was similar to trying to drop clothespins into a milk bottle.

The weather was terrible and we experienced St. Elmo's fire for almost the entire flight. St. Elmo's fire is a phenomenon caused by rain generating static electricity on the aircraft windshield. The result is rivulets of fire streaking erratically up the windshield. I concentrated to keep from getting vertigo the entire flight and on recovery I flew what I would have considered, under normal circumstances, to be a poor approach. Because fighters burn more fuel and are more fuel critical than the other aircraft in the Air Group, they are always recovered first. Also, since Felix and I were the only fighters airborne, we were first in the pattern. The recovery weather was reported to be: pitching deck, 32-48 knots of wind with a left crosswind, 800 ft. overcast, and rain showers. I recall breaking out of the clouds at about 500 feet. The pitching deck was as bad as I have ever seen. When an aircraft carrier is pitching in heavy seas the angled landing runway appears to move in a corkscrew fashion. Normal hook to ramp clearance in an F-4 when the aircraft is centered on glide slope is ten feet. When the deck is pitching, all you can do is average everything out and hope that everything comes together at the right place and at the right time. On this approach, the LSO said, "You're a little low and a little slow."

I distinctly remember thinking "But I'm steady so I'm not changing a thing."

The LSO would later debrief: "Low and slow to climbing". Crossing the ramp, I went for it, blowing a tire and tearing off one of the landing gear doors. Under other circumstances, I would have been disappointed with my performance, but this night I considered myself fortunate and was glad to be aboard. Losing the landing gear door was a normal occurrence when blowing a tire on the F-4.

Just as I taxied clear of the landing area, the undercast lit up and I could see a look of terror on the faces of the flight deck crew as they ran for safety. Looking over my left shoulder, I watched as an A-4, canopy down, skidded down the angle deck and into the water. The pilot was unable to eject and was clearly visible as his aircraft passed by the left side of my F-4. The vivid image of him remains with me to this day. The wing tanks and other remnants of the aircraft continued burning on the flight deck, as the flight deck crew broke out fire hoses to extinguish the fire. In a few minutes, a flight director returned and directed me to taxi forward on the straight deck where I parked the aircraft on the port side of the ship. It was then, before I climbed out of the cockpit, that I experienced a sudden deep wave of nausea.

LT Drex Bradshaw, our squadron LSO, was on the LSO platform at the time of the recovery. During de-brief I asked him exactly what happened. He said that the weather was so bad that they could not tell from the LSO platform, but on a playback of the films of the approach they determined that just as the A-4 pilot dipped his wing for a line-up correction, the wind gusted to fifty knots and the wing tip of the aircraft contacted the flight deck, flipping it to an inverted position as it skidded down the flight deck, off the angle, and into the water. Although the plane guard destroyers searched for remnants of the aircraft, there was no chance of recovering the pilot.

President Johnson called a moratorium on the bombing of the North, so we took a break and headed for Yokosuka, Japan for Christmas. In my opinion, the break was just what the North

Vietnamese needed to rearm and reposition their anti-aircraft and surface-to-air missile defenses.

We returned to the Tonkin Gulf and, after a few days of close air support down South, the moratorium ended. We resumed bombing the North on January 30, 1966. The day we resumed bombing in North Vietnam was the occasion of my forty-seventh mission. I was one of a flight of three F-4s assigned a mission of armed reconnaissance. Approximately seventy miles inland from the coast, west of the city of Vinh, I spotted a bridge that was partially hidden in the foliage below. I called to the other aircraft and armed my bombs. My bomb load consisted of snake eye bombs, a bomb that had retarded fins and required a fifteen degree dive angle. As I rolled in on a west to east heading, I felt a thump and immediately one of my hydraulic flight control warning lights illuminated indicating that I had lost hydraulic fluid in that particular system. Because the aircraft I was flying had a hydraulic flight control failure on the previous flight, I initially assumed that the system had failed once again, and since I was already headed eastward toward the Tonkin Gulf, I continued my dive towards the target. In a matter of seconds my aircraft warning panel lit up like a Christmas tree, and it was apparent that I had taken a hit from anti-aircraft fire. It has been said that "it isn't the anti-aircraft fire that you see that you need to be concerned about; it's the anti-aircraft fire that you don't see that is the concern." I had not seen the anti-aircraft bursts. I jettisoned my bombs and began to dump the fuel in the wings. From the nature of the lights, it was apparent that I had a fire of some kind in the right wing of the aircraft and I wanted to get rid of as much fuel as I could before it had a chance to ignite.

All carrier-based aircraft are designed to fold their wings. This is so that they will take up less space when parked together on the flight or hanger deck. I think the warning light that concerned me most was the "right-wing unlock" light, for I could imagine the right wing folding and the aircraft beginning to tumble. As anxious as I was to reach the coast, I was fearful that if I went supersonic, the aircraft might come apart.

Having notified the rest of the flight as to my situation, I told Joe Stineman, my RIO, that there was nothing more I could do, so if he knew how to pray, he'd better start now! Joe had recently graduated from Notre Dame, and I figured that anyone who graduated from that institution surely ought to know how to pray.

I had never questioned the existence of God, for reason had dictated that where there are order and form, there has to be a creator. I have never seen an aircraft that didn't have a designer or a building that didn't have an architect and a builder. I need only to look at something as intricate as the human eye or watch the sunrise every morning and see it set every evening to realize that, here too, there had to be a master designer or planner. However, the only time I prayed was when I was in real trouble or wanted something really badly. I knew I was in real trouble.

I honestly was not afraid of dying. I had considered the prospect of death many times before I went into combat and, in reality, I was not afraid of dying. However, I did have good friends who were being held in prison camps in North Vietnam and I knew that our government was not doing anything to get them out. I believed that if I were captured, I would be on my own, and there was no way that I wanted to spend a major portion of my life in a stinking North Vietnamese prison camp. Knowing that I had done everything I could to bring the situation under control, I did the only thing that I knew left to do. I began to pray. "Now I lay me down to sleep" just didn't seem to fit the situation. I remembered the Lord's Prayer, for I had prayed it in church as a boy, and before football games as part of the football team in high school. Somehow, that just didn't seem to fit the situation either, so I simply prayed, "Please, God, if you are there, help me. I don't want to be a POW and I surely would like to see my wife, Ann, and our two little girls again."

There was an overcast cloud layer, so I couldn't see the coastline, but we could map the coastline on the radar. Those seventy miles were the longest flight I have ever flown. I have since been asked, "How long did it take?" to which I have replied, "about ten years." Once we cleared the coastline, everything else would be rather anticlimactic. The other two aircraft in our flight had caught up with me and they reported that I had three holes about the size of beer cans in my right wing. I later concluded that I had taken hits from 37MM anti-aircraft guns, but the rounds had not detonated. If the rounds had detonated, they would surely have taken off the wing.

Once I had cleared the coastline and was far enough out to sea so that the North Vietnamese could not pick me up in the event that we had to eject, I breathed a huge sigh of relief. I had established radio contact with the ship and informed them that I wanted them to recover me last so that if I crashed on the flight deck, I wouldn't delay the recovery of the other aircraft. Even though I had lost my utility hydraulic system which was used to operate the landing gear, flaps, and brakes, I had backup pneumatic bottles that would still allow me to lower the gear and flaps. I didn't need brakes since I would be flying an arrested landing and then immediately connected to a tug. I descended to 10,000 feet and, as I slowed the aircraft in anticipation of lowering the flaps, the control stick went hard over to the left. The remaining hydraulic flight control system was still indicating good hydraulic pressure, but because of the electrical fire, I knew the gage was inaccurate. It became obvious that I had lost the hydraulic fluid in the other system and no longer had flight controls. Uncontrollably the plane began turning back toward the coast of North Vietnam, so I promptly told Joe to eject. He responded, "What?", but then he heard me on the radio telling the ship that I was ordering my RIO to eject. I wanted to ensure that Joe was safely out and well clear of the aircraft before initiating my own ejection. Since each crewmember had to initiate his own firing sequence, if care was not taken to personally time each initiation, there was the risk of one's canopy or seat hitting the other canopy or seat after leaving the aircraft. We had lost one of our squadron's RIOs on our first cruise under just such conditions.

The F-4 has a boundary layer control system that routes high-stage bleed air through ducts from the engine to the wing. When the flaps are extended this hot air assists the laminar flow of air across the top of the wing allowing the aircraft to fly at slower speeds during the approach. The pilot on that first cruise reported a boundary layer control leak right after his cat shot and began an immediate turn downwind for recovery. At the ninety-degree position the duct ruptured and hot boundary layer control air ignited his wing fuel. The pilot ejected and was recovered but his RIO didn't make it. All they recovered were parts of his seat and parts of his hardhat.

The F-4 had a Martin-Baker seat with a face curtain ejection handle and an alternate handle between the legs. In the Navy, the face curtain was used primarily to initiate the firing of his seat because it ensured that one was properly positioned, with the head back against the seatback to minimize the risk of spinal injury during the ejection. The last look at my instruments told me that I was at about 10,000 feet and at approximately 220 knots. I don't think that I could have been in a better flight envelope for ejection.

Once I knew Joe was out and clear of the aircraft, I put my head back and pulled the face curtain. The canopy immediately blew and I remember a pause long enough to make me begin to wonder if the rest of the sequence was going to work as designed. I could see just past the right edge of the face curtain and watched the metal frame of the windscreen as I waited for the seat to ignite.

Suddenly there was a loud bang and a swift kick. I immediately experienced a tumbling sensation and some disorientation as I hit the slipstream. Since the main chute is controlled by a barostat and programmed to deploy at 10.000 ft., my chute opened immediately, initiating seat separation. Following the noise created by canopy separation and ejection into the airstream, the silence of hanging in the chute seemed remarkably pleasant. My first impulse was to look up and when I did, I could see that beautiful silk canopy. After removing my oxygen mask, I threw away what was remaining of my pilot's kneeboard, and removed my leather gloves. The gloves would get slippery when wet, so by removing them, I would ensure that I could activate the quick release fittings on my harness and get rid of my parachute on entering the water. My next impulse was to turn to see if I could see Joe and tell if he had a good chute. Pulling the risers, I was able to start a turn. I caught one glimpse of our aircraft, which was now in rapid descent, and then I could see Joe's chute off in the distance. Several aircraft flew by, so I gave them a "thumbs up" to let them know that I was okay. I did check my watch so I could later enter my chute time in my pilot's logbook. My descent took about seven minutes.

I hate snakes. People who know me best know that I have a morbid fear of them and as I descended, I began to think about those large brown, notoriously venomous sea snakes that I had observed from the flight deck of the carrier while it was cruising in the Tonkin Gulf. My seat pan, to which I was still attached, contained a life raft that could be deployed by activating a release handle on the right side of the pan. It worked as advertised and the raft inflated falling below, still attached to my seat harness by a lanyard. I thought about pulling the raft up under me so that when I landed in the water I would already be sitting in the raft and the snakes would be unable to reach me. But then I thought, "What if I just go through the bottom of the raft on impact? Then I won't even have a raft to get into and away from the snakes."

At sea, there were scattered clouds at 2000 feet so when I passed the clouds, I knew it was time to prepare for entry. I had already inflated my life jacket so when I hit the water, I didn't bob much below the surface. By the time I had entered the water, released my chute, and swum clear, a rescue helicopter was overhead. I didn't even have time to climb into my raft. In a matter of minutes, I was on my way back to the ship. Upon arrival, back aboard ship, I was sent to sickbay for observation. The flight surgeon, Ben Bowen, who was a friend of mine, paid me a visit. "You don't spend that much money every day," he said as he handed me some medicinal brandy. The next day I did experience some sore muscles, but apart from that, the worst thing that I suffered from the ejection was a bad hangover and headache from the brandy.

I was allowed to send Ann a telegram. I suppose they knew that there might be a press release and they wanted her to be able to hear from me before reading something in the paper. Desiring to keep it as light as possible, my telegram read: "Had to eject in the vicinity of the ship. Everything worked as advertised and Joe and I are both fine. A letter will follow with details. All my love. Fritz."

I spent the next day gathering equipment to replace what I had lost in the ejection. We were scheduled to proceed to Subic Bay for a five-day break, and I was eager to get back on the horse that had thrown me, so I asked to be put back on the flight schedule. Two days after my ejection and the day before we departed Yankee Station, I flew three missions.

One day, prior to our deployment as I was walking the flight line, I spotted a young airman jumping up and down on one of our aircraft seat pans. This is the seat pan containing the raft and survival equipment. Asking him what in the world he was doing, he responded that he was just trying to get it closed. I immediately collared him and took him to see the Line Division Chief. The line chief assured me that we would shortly be deploying and at such time he would be assigned to ship's company. When the

Air Group joins the carrier, personnel are assigned to the ship's company to assist in routine tasks such as mess cooking.

Whenever a pilot ejects it is customary to reward at least two people with not only a thank-you but also a bottle of their favorite beverage. Those two people would be the pilot who piloted the rescue helicopter and the person who packed your parachute. You can imagine my surprise when I visited the para-loft only to discover that the man who packed my chute was none other the young man that I had reprimanded prior to our deployment.

My friend, Charlie Plumb who was my squadron replacement for the next deployment, was subsequently shot down and captured. As a motivational speaker, Charlie has a wonderful message titled "Who Packed Your Chute?". If you have a chance to hear his message or read his book, *I'm No Hero*, it is well worth the time.

We usually spent about five weeks on station, then five days in port. While on station, we averaged one and a half missions per day. In addition to the combat missions, we manned aircraft in a "ready" status on the flight deck. Typically, we had no more than five hours free of duties, so sleep was catch-as-catch-can within those five hours. Each mission required an intelligence briefing as well as a flight brief, and that was followed by an intelligence debrief upon return.

February through May, I flew a total of eighty-seven additional missions. I was hit several more times by anti-aircraft fire but still managed to get back to the ship. On one of those occasions, I was flight leader of two F-4s. Our assigned target was an army barracks in North Vietnam. My roommate for two cruises, Bill Blunt, had fulfilled his obligated service and departed for home. My new roommate was LCDR John Holmes. Even though John was senior in rank, since he had just arrived, I was the designated flight leader. I planned to proceed at a lower altitude from the coast-in point (the point where we cross the coast) and then fly on the east side of a mountain ridge that ran northeast until we were just east of the assigned target. That way that we could surprise the enemy by lighting the afterburners and popping up to a roll-in altitude sufficient for a forty-five-degree dive to release point. The F-4 aircraft engines left a black trail of smoke which could easily be seen and used for target tracking by those on the ground manning anti-aircraft guns. By lighting the afterburners, we were able to extinguish the black trail. I had no question that our attack would surprise the enemy. Since I would be able to view the target in my rearview mirrors while pulling off the target, I planned to do so in order to give bomb damage assessment on my return to the ship. As I began my pullout and turn to the right, I could see tracers from automatic weapons as they whizzed past my canopy. I quickly decided against getting my own damage assessment and proceeded to climb out to the west.

It was standard procedure to then join up so we could each inspect the other aircraft and determine if we had incurred any damage. I looked John's aircraft over reporting no damage and he, in turn, looked me over reporting the same. I soon realized that my aircraft was requiring an unusual amount of trim. From the cockpit of the F-4, the wingtips of the aircraft are just visible in the rearview mirrors. Looking at my right wing I could see that a large section of it was missing. The leading edge and trailing edge lights were still there but it looked like someone had taken a huge bite out of the wingtip. When I landed back aboard, we found multiple bullet holes starting just aft of the canopy. They had passed through the fuselage and the engines but never hit a fuel line. John Holmes said that as I popped up for my bombing run the tracer rounds from automatic weapons looked like a halo around the aircraft. I ribbed John of course for his failure to see the combat damage, but since it was his first strike mission, I could understand what he must have been experiencing. On another occasion, I returned from a mission with a hole in my flaps. I developed an unenviable reputation for attracting flak. The fighter pilot nickname I received for my ability to attract anti-aircraft fire is not one worth mentioning here.

I often wondered, "How did they know we were coming?" No matter how carefully we planned our approach to the target, it seemed that the enemy was always waiting for us. All of the targeting was being done by President Lyndon Johnson and Secretary of Defense Robert McNamara right from the White House. It would be years later that I learned Secretary of State Dean Rusk would release to the North Vietnamese, through the Swiss Embassy, what the targets would be for the next day. This supposedly was to reduce the chance of collateral damage to the civilian population and avoid injuring any Russian advisors. Where was the concern for our country's own pilots and crewmen? This is inconceivable to me and should have been called treason.

The most meaningful mission for me was a close air support mission south of the DMZ. We were called out one day to provide air support for some troops pinned down on a road by an enemy machine gun emplacement that was in the crevice of a mountainside. We were under the control of a forward air controller who described the target and marked it with smoke. Since there was no anti-aircraft fire, our flight of four F-4s set up a racetrack pattern and I planned a thirty-degree dive angle with a bomb release at 3000 feet. Once again, we were armed with four 250 lb. banded lug bombs. If we were going to help the troops at all, our bombing was going to require pin-point accuracy.

On my first pass, I realized you couldn't even see the crevice until you were right at release altitude. As I flew around the pattern, I could see the hits of the other aircraft, and they were not even coming close. I may have come close, but after three passes I was down to my last bomb and had still failed to hit the target. I determined that on my fourth pass, unless I felt that everything was right on, I wouldn't even release. It wasn't perfect, so I pulled off the target and went around for one more run. The next pass was right on so I released on schedule. The cheering and hollering of the forward air controller gave me my answer; I had hit the target and taken out the machine gun. This was my most meaningful mission because for once I knew that I had saved lives rather than taken lives.

On another occasion, I was flying wing for the Carrier Air Group Commander, Royce Williams, when we ran into some moderate anti-aircraft fire. I had begun a turn to evade when I spotted a dreaded SAM missile as it ignited on the pad. Although I had never seen a SAM in flight, it was unmistakable. It quickly became apparent that it was headed straight for me. Even though we were only at 5000 feet, I rolled inverted and dove for the deck. My heart was in my throat and I couldn't even tell my RIO until after I had established my evasive maneuver. When I rolled out, I was so close to the deck that a farmer could have hit me with his rake. I looked over my left shoulder just in time to see a huge fireball as the SAM detonated on ground contact. The SAM is radar guided and I had managed to get low enough to break the radar track and scrape the SAM off on the terrain. The fireball appeared to be within one hundred yards of our aircraft.

Royce Williams was one of the finest officers I had ever met. Later during the deployment, he was physically grounded and could no longer fly as a pilot. He chose to climb into the back seat and to fly with me as my RIO. I had such respect for him that

I would have followed him anywhere. Years later I would learn of his exploits in the Korean conflict as a young fighter pilot. He attacked seven Soviet MiGs and shot down four of them while flying F9F-5 *Panthers*. His heroics were classified because the Soviets were flying secret missions against NATO and U.S. Forces. Captain E. Royce Williams was truly a forgotten hero in a forgotten war.

The mission that stands out foremost in my mind was the Alpha Strike on the Hai Duong Bridge. The Hai Duong Bridge was an over-under highway and railroad bridge between Hanoi and Haiphong. It had been designated a primary target for quite a while and had been assigned for previous Alpha Strikes, to both the Navy and the Air Force. I can't remember the exact numbers, but I seem to recall between the Navy and Air Force about eleven pilots and twenty-three aircraft had been lost in previous attempts to destroy this particular bridge. At the time the only bridge that had a comparable reputation was the Haiphong Bridge. Because the Rules of Engagement restricted our bombing to lines of communication and transportation, we became primarily bridge bombers. The North Vietnamese knew our restrictions so they concentrated their anti-aircraft guns around their most important bridges. What makes a bridge a particularly difficult target is that your best chance of hitting it with a stream of bombs is to cross it with about a twenty-degree cut. If you were to drop your bombs on a run perpendicular to the bridge, you are likely to drop a bomb on either side of it. If you were to drop on a run parallel to it and there was a crosswind, the bombs would make ground contact on the downwind side. Flying a twenty-degree cut means that you will be flying directly into the anti-aircraft emplacements that are located on both sides of the river and both sides of the road.

Our strike was to be comprised of four A-6 *Intruder* aircraft each carrying four two-thousand-pound bombs, two F-4 *Phantoms* each carrying four one-thousand-pound bombs, and four F-4 *Phantoms* loaded down with 2.75 air-to-ground rockets. In addition to their bombing load, each F-4 carried their normal air to air missile load of two heat-seeking Sidewinder missiles and four radar guided Sparrow missiles for air defense against enemy MiG fighters.

We briefed and manned aircraft several times before we finally had weather at the target good enough to proceed. For me, the hardest part of every mission was the anticipation, so for this particular mission I had to endure that anxiety more than once. When the call "pilots man your aircraft" came, all anxiety subsided and I was completely focused on the task at hand.

We briefed to proceed to the coast at altitude and then descend to between four and six thousand feet line abreast in a combat spread. The lower altitude was chosen because it was above small weapons range and below the altitude that would afford SAM missiles the best chance of gaining a hit. The combat spread gave each aircraft room to jink, rapidly change altitude and heading, to avoid anti-aircraft fire. The A-6s were at the center of the loose formation, the F-4s that were carrying the rockets were on the left side, and the two F-4s carrying bombs were on the right side of the A-6s. The plan was to fly up the river and upon reaching the target the A-6s would split, two to the left and two to the right, and begin a climb to roll-in altitude. Unlike the Air Force, the Navy's tactic was to spread around the target and all dive on the target at the same time. The first time you did it you thought that there would be one big mid-air collision over the target. However, we operated with the idea that there was a lot of airspace and relatively small aircraft. Our tactic required the anti-aircraft gunners to spread their fire over a wide range rather than just aiming their guns in one direction. As the A-6s popped up to the left, the F-4s with rockets were to turn under the A-6s in a spread, scattering 2.75 rockets across the entire area for flak suppression. Since the bombers to the right were spreading around the target and I was on the far right, it meant that I would probably be the last one in and have the most exposure. I had briefed my RIO, Fred Nutting, to call out altitudes on the way up, dive angle when I was in my dive, "fast" or "slow" so I could adjust my release altitude, and then a "standby" and a "mark" at our release altitude of 4000 feet. With these inputs from my RIO, I could completely keep my eyes on the target. I planned to light the afterburners, climb to 10,000 feet, roll inverted, establish my dive angle of forty degrees, then roll out and track the target.

As we reached the bridge, we began our turn and climb to altitude. I had seen 37mm and 57mm anti-aircraft fire before, but this was the first time that I had seen 85mm and 100mm bursts.

37mm bursts leave white puffs of smoke and 57mm leave puffs of gray. 85mm and 100mm are bright orange fireballs accompanied by clouds of black smoke. As I was climbing, I sighted the bridge and could already see the A-6s' bombs contacting the ground. Unfortunately, the ones that I could see were all falling short of the bridge. The anti-aircraft bursts were so intense that passing 9000 feet. I knew that if I stayed at altitude any longer, we would never make it. I rolled inverted at about 9300 feet and rolled out in my dive. I could not have asked for a better track. I was tracking the bridge right to left with a twenty-degree cut. As I looked through my gun sight, the automatic weapons tracers looked like St. Elmo's fire on my windscreen. The air flow across the windscreen seemed to be deflecting the automatic weapons fire. The thought that raced through my mind was, "I know I'm dead so I'm going to get that stinking bridge." Just as I released my bombs and started my pull-out, I spotted an F-4 as he flew under the nose of my aircraft. I had the horrible thought that I may have just dropped my bombs on one of the flak suppression F-4s as he passed underneath my aircraft. My concern was unfounded, as all of our aircraft made it safely back to the ship.

Our G limit on the F-4 was six positive and four negative G's. On my pullout, my accelerometer registered ten G's. Once we had delivered our ordnance, our brief called for joining another aircraft and speeding to the coast. The reason for joining up with another aircraft was so there would be someone to report if and where your aircraft went down.

More than a week passed before a photo-recon aircraft could get pictures of the bridge. When the pictures came in, photos showed that the two center spans of the four spans of Hai Duong Bridge were in the river. I didn't know it then, and wouldn't know until many months later when I was flying test flights in St. Louis, that I had been recommended for and received the Distinguished Flying Cross for my part in the Hai Duong Bridge Alpha Strike.

I was due for orders to shore duty and had requested post-graduate school at Monterrey, Ca. I knew I would need a graduate degree if I were going to eventually be promoted to Admiral, and that first shore duty tour seemed like a good time to get my degree. When the selection list came out, I was on it. However, now coming right out of combat, since I just didn't feel like I would be in a frame of mind to study, I declined. My new orders were even better. I was assigned to be an acceptance test pilot at McDonnell Aircraft in St. Louis, Missouri, testing the new F-4s for the Navy, Marine Corps, and the Air Force. Not only would I continue to build flight time in the world's greatest fighter, but I could go to night school at St Louis University and get the Master's degree that I would eventually need for higher promotion. I had orders for my next duty station, but the skipper informed me that I would be staying until the last day of combat. His concern was if we lost more pilots, the squadron might not be able to get a replacement.

Achieving Centurion- one hundred traps on one ship- was considered a big deal. I had already reached triple centurion status on the Kitty Hawk, and the skipper came to me one day and said, "Fritz, if I give you some additional night missions, you have a chance of making night centurion." I told him that I couldn't care less about night centurion. I just wanted a chance to get home alive. When I departed the Kitty Hawk, the day after we left Yankee Station for the last time, I had 356 traps, including ninety-nine night traps.

I flew the very last mission from the Kittyhawk before the ship left Yankee Station to return home. The day after our departure, I was flown to Kadena AFB Okinawa, and then to Tachikawa AFB in Japan. From there, I boarded a Military Air Transport flight for the final leg to Travis AFB in California.

# CHAPTER 6

Arriving at Travis Air Force Base, within forty-eight hours after I had flown my last mission, we were met by an Air Force Major. Boarding the aircraft, he greeted us with- "Welcome home. If you need transportation, you will have to catch a cab or hitchhike. The buses are on strike." Well, so much for a warm welcome home for returning warriors.

I managed to get to San Francisco International and fly down to San Diego to join Ann and my two little girls, and since Ann had already met with the movers and had our belongings packed and on the way to St. Louis, we immediately began driving east.

Our first visit was with my folks in New Orleans. While we were there, a reporter from the newspaper called. He had learned that I had been shot down and had just returned. He wanted to know if I would do an interview.

During the course of the interview, he asked if I had heard about the draft card burners and, if so, what I thought. I responded that I had read about them in the armed forces newspaper, *Stars and Stripes*, and with all the wisdom of a twenty-seven-year-old fighter pilot, I added that they should be recruited into the Peace Corps and sent to Southeast Asia with shovels. It wouldn't be long before they would want to turn in their shovels for rifles. The next morning, the *New Orleans Times-Picayune* featured a picture of me with Ann and our girls with the bold headline "Vietnam

Veteran Has Novel Idea for Draft Card Burners". Ann received an obscene phone call early that same morning, and my parents continued to receive harassment calls at all times of the night for about six months.

The tour at NAVPLANTREPO in St. Louis was everything I could have wished it to be. The flying was terrific. We would take an aircraft out for its first test flight and really wring it out. An initial flight took about an hour and fifteen minutes, during which time we would operate every system on the plane. Our acceptance flight included a high-speed run and a high "Q" maneuver to see if the aircraft would hold together.

On the first test flight for a new airplane, we would fly two intercepts outbound from St. Louis, evaluating the airborne fire control systems. We then completed a high speed run inbound, invariably achieving an airspeed of greater than Mach 2, twice the speed of sound. At the completion of the speed run, in order to test the aircraft's overall integrity, I would slam the throttles to idle and roll into ninety degrees of bank, pulling as many G's as our airspeed and altitude allowed. Following deceleration, we checked the air-to-ground bombing systems by making bombing runs on designated targets, such as a bridge on the Missouri River. If we were flying a photo recon aircraft, it was necessary to evaluate the low-level sensors of the aircraft's terrain avoidance radar. This was a free ticket to flat hat. What pilot could ask for more? On return, we were met by the subcontractors and debriefed systems deficiencies. Subsequent flights only required retesting systems that had failed the initial flight, so the rest of the flight time was ours to enjoy as we pleased. This was at the height of the F-4D deliveries to the Air Force, and in one month alone we bought eighty-nine airplanes. We were big-time spenders! Although we did buy some aircraft on the initial flight, it normally took an average of three and a half flights before we would complete acceptance.

The only drawback to my enjoyment at this time was reading the messages about air combat losses in Vietnam. With each message I read, I grieved over the death or capture of another airman. I knew firsthand the frustrations of the pilots because of the ridiculous rules of engagement. I also knew that the war was being micro-managed by Lyndon Johnson and Robert McNamara. My anger and frustration over our nation's "no win" policy continued to build.

Returning home at the end of the day, I would go straight to the basement, where I attempted to work off the anger by lifting weights. After a vigorous physical workout, a shower and a couple of drinks, I was finally able to communicate with Ann and my two precious daughters. Ann couldn't understand. She felt we had survived my combat tour and should have every reason to enjoy all that we now had. In retrospect, my family may have been better off if I had just gone to a bar and started a fight instead of bringing my anger and moodiness home. I know now that I was experiencing post-traumatic stress disorder. PTSD was not identified at that time. It would more readily have been identified as depression, but you don't tell a twenty-seven-year-old fighter pilot that he's depressed. It just doesn't fit the image. Combat decorations continued to come in, so at work I was a resident hero. At home, I was just an old grouch.

We tend to think of the effective losses due to combat only in terms of those who lose their lives on the battlefield. Many times, the consequences of trauma are never considered. I lost several friends during this period, and I now realize that their deaths may have been attributed to PTSD and the destructive behavior that normally accompanies it. My first RIO, Mike

Murphy, turned in his wings after our first deployment and was replaced by Dave Coker. Dave flew with me until he was assigned to our new Executive Officer. He then completed a second combat deployment, and subsequently died in an auto accident after "happy hour", while driving from Point Mugu NAS to Los Angeles. Fred Nutting flew with me after Joe Stineman had injured his leg. Fred also experienced an aircraft ejection and after a second combat cruise, died in an accident while riding his motorcycle. My friend, Ed Gross, received orders from St Louis to VF-114. Following a combat cruise on the *Kitty Hawk*, he received orders to be an exchange pilot with the Air Force. He was killed when he hit a bridge abutment in his Porsche.

I knew that while in combat I had become addicted to the rush of adrenalin and often found myself doing things to satisfy my craving for that rush. I would fly down the Mississippi River at or below the levees. I also found myself driving home at high speeds, weaving dangerously in and out of traffic. I believe that it was solely by God's grace that I, too, did not become a PTSD fatality. I put unreasonable demands on my poor wife to try to meet my need for excitement.

We could only fly test flights when the weather was good. The final assembly line for the F-4 was next door to our office, so when the weather was unsuitable for test flying, I enjoyed walking the assembly line. When I walked the production line, I could see the aircraft systems before the skin was applied. As I studied the systems and recalled the location of the anti-aircraft hits I had taken the day I was shot down, I finally had to conclude that, from an engineering standpoint, there was no way that that particular aircraft had continued to fly on its own. I didn't share my thoughts with anyone, not even Ann. I was, however, absolutely convinced that God had spared my life.

This conclusion presented another question; why did God spare me? So many other men had been killed or captured and I thought that they were better men than I was. They were better husbands, better fathers, and better Naval Officers and I just couldn't understand why God had chosen to spare me.

If one were to ask me at that time if I were a Christian, I would have said yes. I wasn't Jewish and I wasn't a Muslim. If asked who Jesus Christ was, I would have said that He was the Son of God, and if further asked what He had done, I would have even responded that He died for me. However, I used to wonder what the big deal was. I knew of a Marine who had thrown himself on a grenade to save his buddies. In reality, I had no idea who Jesus was, or even who He claimed to be. I had what I would have to say was my own personal religion based on the Golden Rule and the Ten Commandments. I reasoned that every time I did something good, I would get a good mark, and every time I did something bad, I would get a bad mark. One day I would come before God, and as long as the scoreboard indicated more good marks than bad, He would say, "You've done okay, you tried really hard, so you can come on into heaven." If I had read the Bible, I would have known differently, but I had never read the Bible. Oh, I had tried to on numerous occasions, especially during my time at Yankee Station. I was given a Bible at the Naval Academy, and I reasoned that anyone who was reasonably intelligent ought to read a book that had been a best seller as long as the Bible had, or that was as widely quoted as the Bible was. I'd pick it up and start right where you'd start any book, right at the beginning. It was a sure-fire cure for insomnia.

I had no answers, but quietly determined to try to be a better person for God. I determined to be a better husband, a better father, and a better Naval Officer. It was kind of like making

New Year's resolutions, but unfortunately, just like New Year's resolutions, it wasn't long before I had broken every one of them.

Six months after my arrival in St. Louis, I determined that I could not sit idly by as our nation's policies in Vietnam continued as they were. Career-wise I had everything going for me. I had a Distinguished Flying Cross, eleven awards of the Air Medal, and the Navy-Marine Corps Commendation Medal for combat. I had completed one hundred and thirty-six combat missions, had three hundred and fifty-six carrier landings and probably had as much flight time in the F-4 as anyone in the Navy. My fitness reports in combat had ranked me one out of 100 of my contemporaries. Nevertheless, I saw no way to deal with my seething anger over the loss of lives and the way the war was being conducted. We were not doing anything to win the war in Vietnam and I had to do something on behalf of my friends and classmates who were POWs. The only honorable way that I could protest was to resign my commission. I wrote a letter to the Secretary of the Navy, citing three primary reasons for my resignation. First, I thought a no-win war was unconscionable. I did not believe that, as a senior officer, I could order men into combat where they were not given the means to win. Secondly, because of the micromanaging of the war from the White House, the military commanders were not even given the authority to make tactical decisions, much less strategic decisions on the conduct of the war. Thirdly, I felt that Robert McNamara had set the military back twenty years. He had no concept of *esprit' de corps* and had absolutely no concern nor understanding of the value of morale in the military. His only concern was numbers. He appeared to believe that everything could be expressed in terms of mathematical equations and worked out on a computer. Every competent leader knows the value of morale, and that the power of the human spirit cannot be expressed in mathematical terms. My resignation was to be tentatively accepted one year from the date it was received. My primary concern from that point on became the issue of what I was going to do with the rest of my life. All I had ever considered and worked for was a career in the military.

Initially, I would not even consider a career with an airline, for I had previously considered an airline pilot nothing more than a glorified bus driver. I dismissed the idea of med school because I couldn't stand the sight of blood. I looked at various opportunities that might offer a chance for advancement to upper-level management and most seriously considered working for IBM. However, as time progressed, I knew that I loved flying and if I took a non-flying job, I would be looking for ways to go flying on the weekend. On the other hand, if I accepted an airline job, I would still be flying and would also have time to pursue other interests that might fulfill my search for significance.

In October 1969, I drove to the Great Lakes Naval Station north of Chicago and completed the administrative details of my separation from the Navy. When I returned to St. Louis, my commanding officer was prepared to swear me in with a reserve commission, but I told him I wasn't ready. He handed me a reserve officer's commission and said that when I was ready, to simply stop by a Navy Command and be sworn in. That commission remains unsigned in a file cabinet in my office today. I believed at that time that the willingness to accept a reserve commission would negate my protest. As much as I had always wanted to be a Naval Officer, and as much as I loved the Navy, my decision to resign was a decision based on principle. Since I had made my decision based on principle, I needed to remain true to myself and accept all that my decision entailed.

I really can't say that I wasn't experiencing some sadness over the death of my dream of a Navy career, but I knew that I had made the right decision and never looked back.

I had a class date of December 4 with Delta Airlines, so we had thirty days to visit my family in New Orleans, and Ann's family in Brunswick, before proceeding to Delta's headquarters in Atlanta.

# Wings of
# *Truth*

# CHAPTER 1

# *Taking Off*

Isaiah 40:31 (NKJV)

But those who wait on the LORD
shall renew their strength;
They shall mount up with wings like eagles,
They shall run and not be weary,
They shall walk and not faint.

S tepping into the elevator at the Delta Training Center, I was
greeted by one of my Naval Academy classmates. Eighteen
in my training class of twenty were ex-military pilots, so it was
almost like joining a new squadron.

That first year after our departure from the Navy was
extremely stressful. Ann's little sister, Crista, who was born after
our daughter Denise and before Karen, was in the final stages
of her battle with neuroblastoma, a deadly childhood cancer.
Also, within a month of my reporting to Delta, Denise again
experienced extremely high fevers which had begun when she was
about a year old. Navy doctors had never investigated the cause,
only giving us instructions to put her in a tepid bath and give
her APCs (All Purpose Capsules, the navy version of aspirin).

The doctors we contacted around Atlanta were not accepting new patients. However, we were blessed to find a Cuban refugee physician who determinedly set out to find the cause of Denise's now 106-degree fever. She connected us with Eggleston Hospital, the pediatric entity of Emory University Hospital. Denise was diagnosed with vesicoureteral reflux which required corrective surgery, so while little Crissie was dying, Denise was in the same hospital undergoing surgery.

Seniority means everything to the airline pilot. Base assignment, the particular equipment to be flown, seat position, monthly scheduling, and vacations are all selected and allotted on the basis of seniority. I guess most pilots like this system, but for someone who is highly competitive it gives no incentive to move ahead based on performance. I received a seniority number the day I reported for training. I really didn't know exactly how our numbers were assigned but I was given a number near the last in the class. We were allowed three choices for our initial base assignment and I selected Atlanta, Dallas, and New Orleans. Because of my position in the class I was sent to New Orleans, my last choice.

Upon completion of my initial training, I took our girls to New Orleans while Ann remained in Atlanta to be with her family during Crissie's last days. We stayed with my folks until we had time to find and buy our first home and receive delivery of our furniture and personal goods from St. Louis.

On the plus side, I had ample time away from flying duty with Delta. Since I had been trained as a DC-6/ DC-7 flight engineer and Delta no longer had DC-6 or 7 aircraft at their New Orleans base, I was instructed to wait for a DC-8 engineer class date in Atlanta. I waited two months for that class, and then another two months for flight training.

Initial probation pay at Delta was a paltry four hundred and fifty dollars a month. Determined to remain debt free, I worked at whatever opportunities I could find to supplement my income. In one month, I drove a delivery truck, painted the interior of an office building, worked as a night watchman on the Mississippi River levee, transported a sailboat from Dallas to Jackson, Mississippi, and sold a house as a real estate agent. Many of my contemporaries on the airline supplemented their incomes by flying in the reserves, but as much as it would have helped us, I felt that accepting a reserve commission would have compromised my protest and I remained determined to stand by my decision.

Wanting to make a difference, I did find time to get involved in grassroots politics and became a Republican Precinct Chairman so that I could work for the election of Louisiana's first Republican congressman, David Treen. I believed that the only way we could bring the Vietnam fiasco to a conclusion was to elect Richard Nixon as president. I teamed with another Delta pilot and we started the Jefferson Parish Young Republicans' Club.

Since we had purchased our first home very near to where I had grown up, we attended the same church where I had gone to Sunday school and church as a boy.

Every Sunday that I was not working, I joined the rest of the family at church. It was important to me to attend services for several reasons. I knew that God had spared my life in Vietnam, and I wanted to pay Him back. One way I felt I could do that was by going to church.

When our first little girl, Denise, arrived, the thought of raising a little girl scared me to death, because I know how little boys think. And now, having two little girls, I wanted them to have the moral guidance of Sunday school and church until they were old enough to weigh the consequences of the decisions they would be making. In addition, I felt that attending Sunday services simply suited the image that I determined I should have.

Not only did I attend church, I became quite active. I volunteered to teach Sunday school and became my younger brother Mike's Sunday school teacher. I was given a lesson book, so I prepared each lesson directly from that material. I remember asking the Sunday school superintendent if there was not some additional material that I might use to better prepare. She could not offer any suggestions, and I have since wondered why she didn't suggest that I might try reading the Bible.

In addition to teaching Sunday school, I served on the Administrative Board and the Commission for Evangelism. When asked to join other men in visiting those who had attended a service, I readily found an excuse. I felt that there was no good reason I could ask someone to go to church with me. If they had a golf game going or enjoyed fishing on Sunday morning, they had more than what I had.

Sensing that there was some spiritual element missing in my life, even though I had been a member for many years, I attended a new members class. I was given an essay by theologian Paul Tillich. His essay left me even more dissatisfied for it made no sense at all. At the conclusion of the class, I simply assumed that there was really no more to Christianity than what I already knew.

I was spiritually bankrupt, and the sad thing is that I assumed that there was no one who called themselves a Christian who had any more than what I had.

One day I received a visit from the associate pastor. He asked me, "What do you think the purpose of life is?" I couldn't give him a meaningful answer. I told him that I suppose it was to take care of my family. He offered no further suggestions. I now say that there are three major questions that any thinking person would have to ask themselves at some time or other: where did I come from, why am I here, and where am I going? In answer to the first, I had no answer beyond that I came from my mother's womb. To the second question I would say, to take care of my family and, perhaps, to leave the world a better place than when I first arrived. In answer to the third, my only response was that I hoped that I would go to heaven.

In retrospect, I now conclude that I was in a state of deep depression, and was fighting to grab onto anything that would help me keep my head above water. I used activity to try to hold the tide at bay, but fight as I may, I kept sinking deeper and deeper. I had a faithful wife, but I was unable to even see and accept the fact that she still loved me. I had lost all sense of meaningful purpose. I had worked for the election of Richard Nixon and Spiro Agnew, both of whom were removed from office for corruption and cover-up. My country's military leaders had let me down and now I realized that those whom I had worked to put in office were all motivated by personal gain. As I was flying, I saw and became concerned about environmental pollution. I came to the realization that this world was not going to be here forever.

I did not want any more children because the thought of bringing a child into this dark world was more than I could bear. Ann however, wanted another and the one bright spot in all of this darkness was the birth of our beautiful baby boy. Threatened several times with miscarriage, she fought hard to maintain her pregnancy. I can only thank God for her courage and persistence, for I can't imagine life without Denise, Karen, and Will.

On the airline, I progressed quickly from DC-8 flight engineer to DC-9 co-pilot, and within a couple of years we could afford a move. I felt that a new home and location would be beneficial for the whole family. We could try to move to a different pilot base, which would be a setback in pay and working conditions, or we could move to the north shore of Lake Ponchartrain. After deciding to move to Covington on the north shore, we found a contractor, a designer, and built a new home. We were soon moved in and looking for a new place to spend our Sunday mornings. We tried several churches before being invited by another Delta pilot and neighbor to visit a little non-denominational church that he was attending. The first Sunday, a substitute Sunday school teacher, an attorney from New Orleans, was teaching evolution versus creation. My initial response was, "This fellow is so far out in left field that he isn't even in the ballpark."

Ann and the children were pleased with the church, and since I flew on many Sundays, I agreed to abide by their choice. They attended regularly and I joined them whenever I wasn't working.

Our regular teacher, Rudy Atkins, was a distributive education teacher at the local high school. He had been a semi-professional baseball player prior to becoming a teacher, and spoke of having a life change while attending a Billy Graham Crusade. On Sundays, he chose to teach verse by verse, page by page, directly out of the Bible. I had never heard anyone teach directly from the Bible. I listened, not so much because I was intent upon the content of what he was teaching, but because he talked so fast, I found it a challenge just to catch the words he was saying.

Over the next six months, I became convinced of several things. First of all, it was evident that this man actually believed what he was teaching. It was also clear that there were others in the class who apparently believed, and those people seemed to have a quality of life that was different from my own. I became less sure that I had any answers at all. Maybe there really was more to Christianity than what I had previously considered.

During this same period, I was finally coming to grips with

the reality that no matter how hard I tried, I could not in my own strength be the person that I had determined to be. I couldn't be the father I wanted to be; I couldn't be the husband I wanted to be; I just couldn't be the person I wanted to be. I have heard it said that if we push hard enough, God will allow us enough rope to hang ourselves, and that was certainly the case with me. I could not even live up to my own personal standards, much less God's standards. I was coming face to face with my own depravity and violated the very principles that were of greatest importance to me personally. I knew that I could lose my family, the thing I held most dear.

Hank McGrew, a former Marine fighter pilot who had flown with the Black Sheep Squadron in the Pacific, and his wife M Jo were in the same Sunday school class. Since they had been in the Sunday school class and church with us before our move to the north shore, we knew who they were. Hank was a guy that you wouldn't want to cross. He would just as soon punch you out as give you the time of day. When the teacher invited members to join him for an event in Dallas, Texas, Hank agreed to fly them to Dallas. It was a kick-off for the "Here's Life" campaign of Campus Crusade for Christ in 1972.

It was the Sunday morning following their return that I was sitting there with Ann by my side, and people were talking about the event they had attended at the Cotton Bowl in Dallas. They seemed to exude an enthusiasm for life like nothing I had ever known. It was clear that something had changed in the lives of both Hank and his wife. Ann turned to me and said, "I don't know what it is they have, but that is what I want." I didn't know what they had either, but I thought that I knew someone who did know what they had- that former semi-pro baseball player. I swallowed a lot of pride that morning and, at the conclusion of the class, I walked up and asked him if he would come by and visit.

The reason I say that I swallowed a lot of pride is because he had tried to come by and visit several times before, but I always had an excuse. We had a favorite pastime in southern Louisiana, and that was eating seafood and drinking beer. I recall one night that I had a fresh sack of oysters. I was busy opening oysters and drinking beer when the telephone rang.

Ann said, "It's the Sunday school teacher. He wants to know if he can come by and visit."

I said, "Tell him I'm not here."

The last person I wanted to see was a Sunday school teacher. You see, I thought that he was peddling religion, and I concluded the one thing I didn't need was religion. If I had realized that what I really needed and what he had were answers to life's greatest questions, perhaps I would have listened. I have yet to meet a man or a woman who doesn't need answers to those very same questions.

He said he would come by one evening during the following week. That week, as I waited for his visit, I felt a sense of anticipation. I realized that I had come to the end of myself. Not knowing what would transpire, it was clear that something needed to change. I needed something that would give me hope that things could be different. I had everything that should have given me happiness. I had a beautiful wife, three wonderful children, and a job flying airplanes, something I loved to do. I had a new home and two new automobiles and, yet, in spite of all the material things, my life was empty. I looked pretty good on the outside, but on the inside I was miserable. All the things that I thought would satisfy had failed to fill the emptiness in the deepest recesses of my being.

The anticipated day of meeting with our Sunday school teacher finally arrived. Ann and I listened to what he had to say, and I heard some interesting things, things I had never seriously considered. He said that the very reason man existed was to have fellowship with God. But because man determined to go his own independent way, fellowship with God was broken. He said that this self-will, which is characterized by active rebellion or simply passive indifference, is evidence of what the Bible calls sin.

That was news to me. I thought sins were things like drunkenness, adultery, murder, and robbery. According to what he was saying, sin is simply a matter of a person acting apart from God or as if God doesn't even exist. I had always been able to convince myself that I was not so bad. Certainly not a person who could be called a "sinner". For the first time I accepted the fact that I was a sinner. I had proven that I was unable in my own strength to be the kind of person I wanted to be, much less than what God wanted me to be.

He explained that the result of sin is death, or separation from God. God is holy and man is sinful and a great chasm or gulf exists between God and man. Man is constantly trying to cross the chasm and close that separation. He does so by trying to live a good life, having a code of ethics, reasoning through philosophy, and even practicing religion. He told us that even religion is simply man's best effort to reach God. However, that poses a dilemma, because man can't reach God. Then he explained the good news. Where I could not reach God, God Himself took the initiative and reached down to me, man, through the person of Jesus Christ. Christ died for my sins, was buried and bodily rose again on the third day. The death, burial, and resurrection of Jesus Christ are not myths or fables, but confirmed facts of history.

For those who would question the validity of the Christian

faith, I would say the real question is "Did a dead man get up and walk?" If one could disprove the fact of the bodily resurrection of Jesus Christ, the Christian faith would be worth nothing, but the historical evidence of the resurrection is indeed profound.

"I have been used for many years to study the histories of other times, and to examine and weigh the evidence of those who have written about them, and I know of no one fact in the history of mankind which is proved by better and fuller evidence of every sort, to the understanding of a fair inquirer, than the great sign which God hath given us that Christ died and rose again from the dead." Thomas Arnold, Oxford University. (*The New Evidence That Demands a Verdict*, Josh McDowell.)

He explained that becoming a Christian was simply a matter of accepting the forgiveness that Jesus Christ has provided for my sin by His sacrificial, substitutionary death on the cross, and then allowing Him to come into my life, taking control, and making me the person He would have me to be.

I considered several things that night. First, I determined that if there was a God, and I did believe there was, I certainly didn't know Him personally. I had tried to know Him ever since I realized that He had spared my life in Vietnam. However, I had always tried to know Him on my own terms. For the first time in my life, I was ready to meet God on His terms. If there was anything more to the business of Christianity than what I knew, I wanted to know it once and for all or else I never wanted to darken the doorsteps of another church.

He told me that I could accept God's forgiveness and invite Jesus into my life by a simple matter of prayer. I prayed that prayer, admitting that I had sinned, thanking Jesus for dying for my sins, and asking Him to come into my life, to take control of my life and make me the person He wanted me to be.

After I had prayed, Rudy asked me where Christ was right then. Seeing that I was puzzled by the question, he showed me from scripture that Christ Himself said, "Behold, I stand at the door and knock. If anyone hears my voice and opens the door, I will come in to him and eat with him, and he with me." Revelation 3:20 (ESV). Believing that Jesus had willingly died for me, I reasoned that certainly He would come into my life if I invited Him. I then lowered my head and thanked Him for forgiving me and coming into my life as Lord and Savior.

Later that night I knelt beside my bed as I had done as a child. This time, however, rather than praying "Now I lay me down to sleep..." I simply prayed, "God, I don't really know how to pray, so I am just going to talk to you."

# CHAPTER 2

# *Climbing Out*

S hortly after my decision to allow Christ to take control of my life, Rudy challenged me to adopt a "Life Verse"; a Bible verse that would convey what I felt was God's direction for me personally. Having already determined that presenting the good news of forgiveness through Christ was the most important thing that I could do for anyone at any time, Romans 1:16, 17(ESV) seemed to capture the essence of God's leading in my life.

It is written, "For I am not ashamed of the gospel, for it is the power of God for salvation to everyone who believes, to the Jew first and also to the Greek. [17] For in it the righteousness of God is revealed from faith for faith, as it is written, "The righteous shall live by faith."

I am not ashamed of the gospel because first of all it is powerful; it has the power to change lives. Secondly, it is universal. It applies to all mankind and can change anyone's life just as it had changed my own. Lastly, it is not the plan of man but the plan of God Himself.

I had tried to change my life many times. I was always looking for the next self-help best seller. I believed that if I could change the external, somehow it would penetrate down and change the internal. All of my efforts were focused on modifying or changing my behavior. Although I looked pretty good on the outside most of the time, I knew very well that I fell far short of living up to the image that I desired: the image that had produced that high school nickname of "Golden Boy". Where my best efforts had failed to transform the inside, the gospel of Christ had supernaturally transformed something inside, and that transformation was slowly working its way to the outside and changing my behavior. When I came across the Bible verse 2 Corinthians 5:17 (ESV) which says, "Therefore, if anyone is in Christ, he is a new creation. The old has passed away; behold, the new has come," I knew that it was clear what had happened to me and how it was impacting my life.

I wish I could say that the outward change was complete, but I am convinced that it will continue to either the grave or to Christ's return, whichever comes first.

It's a good thing that God doesn't allow us to see all at once the areas of our lives that need to be changed. If He did, it would be more than we could bear. I do know that the older I become, the more I realize how depraved I really am. Perhaps it is simply a matter of growing in my intimacy with Christ. The closer I grow in my relationship with Him, the more I see how far short I fall. Romans 8:29(ESV) says, "For those whom he foreknew he also predestined to be conformed to the image of his Son, in order that he might be the firstborn among many brothers." This gives me the assurance that God is and will continue working in my life to make me what He wants me to be.

While I now have a more honest view of my own depravity, I am not overwhelmed, for I also can see how much has changed. It's comforting to know that the changes which have occurred are not a result of my own efforts. They are a result of simply seeking to know Him. These changes are all by His grace alone. When I do fail, I have learned to confess my sin, which is simply a matter of acknowledging and agreeing with God concerning my failure. I

John 1:9(ESV) says, "If we confess our sins, He is faithful and just to forgive us our sins and to cleanse us from all unrighteousness."

When Jesus died on the cross for my sins, I had not yet been born. I accepted His forgiveness the night I surrendered my life to Him and received His forgiveness for sins past, present, and future. So, after agreeing with God concerning my sin, I thank Him for that forgiveness. I am so thankful that my acceptance by God is not based on my performance. You cannot imagine how powerful this truth is to someone who, like me, has always assumed that he could only be accepted based on his accomplishments. I thank God every day that I can know that I will be with Him eternally, and that knowledge is based not on what I do, but on what He has already done. It is God's love for me that compels me when I do fall, to get back up, dust myself off, and move on.

One of the ideas presented in the Campus Crusade "Basic Concepts" was an exercise called "spiritual breathing". This taught that confession was analogous to exhaling. Just as physical exhaling expels the old bad air, confession in turn releases or expels our failure to live up to God's standard as presented in scripture. After exhaling, we can then inhale by asking God to fill us with His Holy Spirit. As Ephesians 5:18(NKJV) reads, "And do not be drunk with wine, in which is dissipation; but be filled with the Spirit." The Holy Spirit comes into our lives at the moment we surrender our lives totally to Christ, and by asking God to fill us with His Spirit, we are able to appropriate, by faith, the power that He provides. God does not ask us to do anything that He does not give us the power and ability to do. His Spirit empowers us to live as He would have us to live.

When I surrendered my life to Christ, I accepted the fact that I would be willing to go wherever he wanted me to go and to do whatever He wanted me to do. This could mean, of course, leaving my flying career with the airline. The thought of leaving my job was not a big deal.

At the moment of my surrender, I said, in essence, "God, You can have my marriage, my family, my bank account, my job. You can have everything. If I can know You, I want to know You and You can have it all." As I strive to communicate my decision to others, I simply say that, "I came out of the cave with my hands up". I believe that this gives a clear picture of complete surrender.

I did consider the possibility of going to seminary or joining a full-time Christian ministry- the Navigators, but as I continued to read my Bible, I came to I Corinthians 7:24(NKJV): "Brethren, let each one remain with God in that state in which he was called." Although God might have made a different vocation or calling clear at some later date, this verse and ones preceding it cautioned me against making a change unless I was certain that He was directing the change. I was content to accept the fact that I was right where He wanted me to be.

We are all tempted to look back at times and ask ourselves, "Should I have done some things differently?" or "Should I have moved here or there?" Another verse that was given to me by Rudy Adkins to memorize was Proverbs 3:5-6(NKJV): "Trust in the Lord with all your heart and lean not unto your own understanding. In all of your ways acknowledge Him and He will direct your path." The challenge for me is to ensure that I am acknowledging Him in all of my ways: my schedule, my thought life, my finances, my relationships, my vocation. If I am doing this, I can rest assured that He is leading me where He wants me to be and to do what He wants me to do.

If one will begin each day by acknowledging that they are available totally to God and willing to follow Him wherever He leads, then they can truly live a life without regrets.

# CHAPTER 3

## *Staying on Course*

G rowing up in a structured home at the hands of a German father and attending military schools from fifth grade insured that discipline from the hands of others was present in my life from an early age. Participation in athletics and having a desire to excel in the classroom later encouraged me to develop a certain amount of self-discipline. While many have a rather negative view of discipline, I see it quite differently. I believe that self-discipline has allowed me to compensate for what I have lacked in natural ability. During my high school athletic days, I would not even partake of a soft drink during sport seasons, because I had heard that it could cause you to be short-winded.

I am now eighty years old and my athletic days are far behind me, but diet and exercise remain a very important part of my life, and remaining physically fit contributes greatly to my overall sense of well-being. I still enjoy regularly working out on the weight equipment at our local sports center. My only other athletic endeavor is golf, a sport in which aggressiveness unfortunately doesn't really help. In golf, older men talk of being able to shoot their age. I'm afraid that the only way I could ever do that is to live to be well over a hundred.

I will forever be grateful to the men who taught and encouraged me to follow the spiritual disciplines of the Christian life. The night I prayed and invited Christ to come into my life, my friend, Rudy, gave me a booklet, *"Beginning with Christ"*, written by the Navigators. This booklet contained four assurance verses, and my friend knew that those four assurances would be essential to my new walk with Christ. The first verse, "Assurance of Salvation", is absolutely critical if one is going to enjoy the abundant life that God intends for everyone who makes the decision to follow Him. I John 5:11-12(NKJV): "And this is the testimony: that God has given us eternal life, and this life is in His Son. He who has the Son has life; he who does not have the Son of God does not have life." It then goes on to say in verse 13(NKJ): "These things I have written to you who believe in the name of the Son of God, that you may know that you have eternal life, and that you may continue *to* believe in the name of the Son of God." If one does not have this absolute assurance, there is no way that he can enjoy life as God intends, for without it he can only go through life questioning his eternal destiny. One thing that has kept me on course is the knowledge that my final destination is assured. I can know without a doubt that when I cross into eternity I will be with God. This assurance is not based upon my performance, but rather on the very character of God Himself. When I fall, it is this assurance that allows me to pick myself up and continue on.

The second verse, "Assurance of Answered Prayer", is John 16:24(NKJV). It says, "Until now you have asked nothing in My name. Ask, and you will receive, that your joy may be full." This verse assures me that my prayers are not simply bouncing off the ceiling. When I pray, I can first of all know that God hears, and secondly, that He will answer. Perhaps the answers are not always in accordance with my timing or exactly the answer that I desire, but nonetheless, I can know that I am being heard.

The third verse, Proverbs 3:5-6 is the "Assurance of Guidance" which I have already discussed. The fourth verse, I Corinthians 10:13(NKJV), is "Assurance of Deliverance". It says, "No temptation has overtaken you except such as is common to man; but God *is* faithful, who will not allow you to be tempted beyond what you are able, but with the temptation will also make the way of escape, that you may be able to bear it." According to God's promise, I can know that whatever temptation I might face is something that others have also faced. God will deliver me, but it is my responsibility to look for the way of escape that He promises to provide. God has demonstrated to me time and time again that if I will look for a way to escape temptation, He can be depended on to provide it.

I was told to memorize these four verses, and they became the foundation of my new walk of faith. Not only was I encouraged to learn these, but I was also challenged to continue to learn other verses. I would like to say that I have always been consistent, but unfortunately, I cannot. Although I have been sporadic in my scripture memorization, I feel that it has been among the most productive things I have ever done, and for that reason, I continue to work at it even today. We must listen to others teach from the Word and we must also read and study Scripture for ourselves, for both are important. However, what we commit to memory, we have with us no matter where we are, and the practice causes us to meditate and process what God says. It allows us to internalize it and find personal application.

In his letter to the Church at Thessalonica, Paul writes: I Thessalonians 5:23(NIV): "May God Himself, the God of peace, sanctify you through and through. May your whole spirit, soul, and body be kept blameless at the coming of our Lord Jesus Christ." This verse tells me first of all that man is a three part being, with a spirit, a soul, and a body. Many recognize a body and soul, but discount the spiritual aspect of their being. Apart from God, man is spiritually dead, and it is only when one comes to God on His terms that man is born spiritually. When approached by Nicodemus, a member of the Jewish ruling council, Jesus declared that, "no one can see the kingdom of God unless he is born again." John 3:3(NIV). When questioned further, Jesus replied that man must be born of water and of the Spirit. My spiritual birth occurred the night I surrendered my life totally to God, and at that moment my spirit was sanctified, or set apart for eternity. My earth suit, on the other hand, continues to decay. It will not be sanctified until I take my last breath and receive my resurrected body.

So, what about the soul? I believe that man's soul is comprised of the mind, the will, and the emotions. If the spirit has already been sanctified and the body will be sanctified at some time in the future, then the sanctification process of which Paul speaks that takes place here on earth must be the sanctification of the soul. The mind is simply an amazingly complex computer, and what we get out of our computer is dependent upon, and no better than, what we program into it. Through newspapers, magazines, television, radio, movies, and the internet, we are constantly bombarded with all kinds of information. How much of what we receive from these sources is truth? If I am going to ensure that I am operating on good data and maintaining right thinking, it is mandatory that I program my computer with truth. The only way I know to do that is to ensure that I am continually hearing, reading, studying, and memorizing the Word of God.

I am convinced that the sanctification of the will began the moment I first surrendered my will to God, and it continues to be sanctified or set apart moment by moment as I choose to submit my will to Him.

I believe that the emotions are sanctified as we learn to walk by faith. Most Christians are okay as long as their circumstances line up with their desires and expectations. It doesn't take much faith to walk a Christian walk as long as things are going our way. However, too many Christians are ruled and guided by their emotions, so when their circumstances no longer align with what feels right, truth gives way to emotion. That is why there are so many divorces among those who profess to be following Christ. I know that emotions lie; there have been times when I have not felt loved, and yet I now know that I was loved. If I respond to what my body tells me, I can also go awry, for my body also lies. How many times have you heard someone say, "I'm starving to death," when one quick glance assures you that they cannot be starving. Every pilot who has experienced vertigo will quickly tell you that if he responds to what his body is telling him and does what feels right, the results can be fatal.

Aviation presents a great metaphor to the principles of walking by faith. Every pilot has experienced vertigo at one time or another. We orient ourselves with our surroundings based on three basic inputs. First are the visual cues to those things around us. Second is the gravitational pull on the joints of the body. Then third, we have the fluid in the semi-circular canal of the inner ear, the movement of which is sensed by tiny hairs sending a signal to the brain that that the body is in motion. As long as none of these is impeded, we are in pretty good shape. But then what happens if we lose one? Say, for instance, the pilot who flies into a cloud bank. He has lost his visual cues outside of the cockpit. Let's then say he begins a slow turn, setting into motion the fluid in the inner ear sending the signal to his brain that he is in a turn. If he then levels his wings, the fluid in the inner ear is still moving, still sending the signal that he is in a turn. If he responds to everything his body is telling him, everything that feels right, he will continue to turn back and one of two things can happen. One, he can tighten his turn until he stalls the aircraft, spins, crashes, and burns, or he can enter an ever-continuing descending spiral called a graveyard spiral, the end of which speaks for itself. I contend that is where most people in our society are today. I believe that they are experiencing spiritual vertigo. Scripture says "There is a way that seems right to a man, but its end is the way of death." In fact, it is so important that it is said twice in the very same words. Proverbs 14:12, Proverbs 16:25(NKJV)

There is one hope or solution for the pilot who is experiencing vertigo, and that is to totally ignore what his senses are telling him and to get his focus back into the cockpit and fly according to his flight instruments, his primary instrument of which is his attitude gyro. I further contend that the primary flight instrument of life is the Word of God. Jesus says, as recorded in John 14:6(NKJV), "I am the way, the truth, and the life. No one comes to the Father except through me." This metaphor of using the Word of God as the primary flight instrument of life applies not only to initially coming to know God in a personal way, but also to continuing to walk by faith. The Apostle Paul in his letter to the Colossians says, "As you therefore have received Christ Jesus the Lord, so walk in Him, rooted and built up in Him and established in the faith, as you have been taught, abounding in it with thanksgiving." Colossians 2:6,7(NKJV)

Years ago, I did a faith study by Manly Beasley in which he asserted that walking by faith is "acting as if it's so, even though it is not so, in order that it may become so, experientially." I love that definition, and Beasley's words have remained with me ever since.

My body can lie; my emotions can lie. The only thing that cannot lie is the Word of God. I therefore believe that my emotions are sanctified by faith as I choose to walk and live in accordance with His Word.

There are many times that I may say to myself, "How can you call yourself a Christ follower, considering what you have done?" I thank God that I can know I am His and He is mine based on my faith and trust in His Word, rather than how I might feel at any given moment.

# CHAPTER 4

# *Progress Reports*
## *A Life of Purpose*

If I were to ask you, "Who is the wisest man who ever lived?", more than likely many of you maybe would say it was King Solomon. As a young man, scripture records that Solomon loved the Lord and walked in the statutes of his father, David. With humility, Solomon asked God for an understanding heart to judge His people and discern between good and evil. God was so pleased with Solomon's request for understanding, to discern justice, that He not only gave him a wise and understanding heart, but gave him also that which he did not request, both riches and honor. (I Kings 3) As a result, King Solomon surpassed all of the kings of the earth in riches and wisdom, and all of the earth sought the presence of Solomon just to hear his wisdom. (I Kings 9:23-24)

If you were to read the book of Ecclesiastes, written by Solomon towards the end of his life, you might ask how someone who started so well could finish so poorly. Solomon may have been the wisest man who ever lived, but to me he is perhaps the most tragic character in all of Scripture.

How can a man who possessed all that Solomon possessed, and accomplished all that Solomon accomplished, come to the end of his life and conclude that all that he has invested his time, talent, and treasure in is pointless? How can he say that his life is meaningless?

The key to understanding the words of Solomon, as recorded in Ecclesiastes, is found in the phrase, "under the sun". If there is no meaning or purpose in life to be found by man "under the sun", then the only hope for finding meaning and purpose must lie in the heavens. There are two vacuums that exist within the life of everyone. The first is in the heart of man, which only God can fill. The French philosopher and physicist, Blaise Pascal, said that every man has a God-shaped vacuum. Men may try to fill that void with whatever they can, but to no avail, because that vacuum is absolutely and unequivocally God-shaped.

The second vacuum exists in the soul of every man. It is a life-sized vacuum of purpose that only a life mission can fill.

The God-shaped vacuum within my heart was filled when I invited Jesus to come into my life: when I humbled myself and surrendered myself totally to Him. I willingly met Him on His terms, allowing Him to have all I possessed. I came out of the cave with my hands up, surrendering all that I was and all that I had.

In I Kings 11:1-4(NKJV), "But King Solomon loved many foreign women, as well as the daughter of Pharaoh: women of the Moabites, Ammonites, Edomites, Sidonians, *and* Hittites— [2]from the nations of whom the LORD had said to the children of Israel, 'You shall not intermarry with them, nor they with you. Surely they will turn away your hearts after their gods.' Solomon clung to these in love. [3]And he had seven hundred wives, princesses, and three hundred concubines; and his wives turned away his heart. [4]For it was so, when Solomon was old, that his wives turned his heart after other gods; and his heart was not loyal to the LORD his God, as *was* the heart of his father David."

Although he started well, Solomon deliberately chose to live "under the sun", rather than living under the principles and precepts given by God. As a result, all of the sweet fellowship Solomon initially had with God turned to bitterness and futility. In the process of gratifying his own passions, Solomon expended all of the resources of the nation Israel on the personal aggrandizement of his own monarchy, and the ultimate outcome of his self-indulgence was a divided kingdom, with all the weakness and misery that followed.

The second vacuum, the life-sized life purpose, can only be filled with a meaningful life mission. It, too, cannot be filled "under the sun". Only looking to the heavens for God to give meaning and purpose to life itself will fill this void. My friend, Joe Coggeshall, challenged me time and time again to find and write a meaningful life purpose and mission statement.

During the ten and a half years I spent in the military, if you had asked me if I knew another Christian, I would have told you I did not. I knew a few guys were suspect because they didn't drink as much as the rest of us, but I had never had another man sit down with me one-on-one and share with me exactly who Jesus was and what that should mean to me personally. Understanding what He did for me and what he had done for others, Romans 1:16-17 seemed to best define my life purpose. Over time, I realized that there was more to life than simply sharing the gospel with others. I came to the realization that knowing God and pursuing intimacy with Him was a life-long process, and whatever else I may do for Him or others must emanate from my personal relationship with Him. Above all, the priority and pursuit of that relationship must come first.

I believe that Solomon did much for God, but because he failed to clearly understand his life purpose and mission, he was distracted and led astray by worldly pursuits and ambitions.

My life purpose and mission today are derived from Matthew 22:36-39(NKJV): "'Teacher, which is the great commandment in the law?' Jesus said to him, 'You shall love the Lord your God with all your heart, with all your soul, and with all your mind. This is the first and great commandment. And the second is like it. You shall love your neighbor as yourself.'"

Since I believe that God's ultimate purpose for all of mankind is encapsulated in these verses, they have become the foundation for my own life purpose. I have derived from it a personal mission statement as well.

"How do you love God?" Realizing all that God had done for me and understanding how much He loved me, I had a natural desire to love Him in return. Even though I expressed my love for Him verbally, I never felt that my love for God was sufficient. I told Him so, acknowledging that a deep love for Him was not something that I could derive from my own efforts, and I certainly didn't want to fake it. I asked Him to help me to love Him more and expressed the desire to be head over heels in love with Him. I even told Him that I wanted to be so much in love with Him that I would be bullet-proof. Later, realizing that there was a selfish motive to the idea of being bullet-proof to life's hurts and pains, I backed away from that idea. I desired to love God enough to want to be satisfied to accept whatever He had for me, even if it was emotionally painful.

In learning to love my wife as God had commanded, I came across a book, *Love Language*, that was most helpful. Realizing that I had always tried to show my love for her in ways that I would perceive love, I learned that her love language was different from my own. If she were ever to understand and accept my love for her, I needed to learn to express that love in ways that she could understand.

If one were asked how they knew God loved them, if they grew up in the church, they would probably cite the phase they learned in Sunday School; "Jesus loves me this I know, for the Bible tells me so." Although this is true, I say that I know God loves me because He came to planet Earth in the form of a man and willfully allowed Himself to be ridiculed, rejected, spat upon, unmercifully beaten, and ultimately have nails driven through his hands and feet as He was hung from a cross. He showed His love for me in a way that I could relate to and understand.

I've discovered that just as each of us have a love language, God has a love language as well. Jesus says in John 14:21(NKJV), "He who has My commandments and keeps them, it is he who loves Me. And he who loves Me will be loved by My Father, and I will love him and manifest Myself to him."

With this in mind, this has become my life purpose, "I will pursue intimacy with Christ above all else, and will endeavor to have a daily quiet time whereby I might read, study, and memorize the Word of God with the intent of bringing all of my being into conformity and subjection to God's commandments as presented in principle and precept in His Holy Scriptures."

As far as loving my neighbor, I know that the greatest and most loving thing that I could do for anyone is to help them to be reconciled to God, that they may know that their sins are forgiven and they can spend eternity with Him. With this in mind, "I will pray for and endeavor to meet the spiritual, emotional, and physical needs of my family in such a way that my efforts will communicate God's unconditional love. I will endeavor to live a life before them that reflects my love for God as well as my love for each one of them personally. I will seize every opportunity to share the gospel of Christ with gentleness and respect with all whom I meet."

In addition to a purpose statement, I have a mission statement that defines my goals. Someone once shared with me that if you are going to set a goal, make it big. They used the term "BHAG"; a big hairy audacious goal. With that in mind, I adopted something that only God could do. My mission statement is, "To change the world by motivating men to unleash the power of the Gospel." The only way we can have a changed world is to have changed men and women, and the only one who can change a man is the Lord Jesus Christ. The gospel is powerful, it is universal, and it is God's plan. It can change anyone just as it changed me. Its power simply needs to be unleashed, and God has given me a heart to try to motivate men to unleash its power by communicating who Jesus is and what is has done for every one of us. "For God so loved the world that He gave His only begotten Son, that whoever believes in Him should not perish but have everlasting life." John 3:16(NKJV)

# CHAPTER 5

# *A Co-pilot*
## *Man's Helper*

The very first reference to God, in the opening words of Genesis, "In the beginning God...." is the Hebrew word Elohim. This word, which is plural, confirms that God is relational. The Father, the Son, and the Holy Spirit have been together from eternity past. Within this relationship, the Trinity, there is unity, equality, roles, authority, and submission.

In Genesis, it is written: "And the Lord God said, 'It is not good that man should be alone; I will make him a helper comparable to him." Gen. 2:18(NKJV)

"And the Lord God caused a deep sleep to fall on Adam, and he slept, and He took one of his ribs and closed up the flesh in its place. Then the rib which the Lord God had taken from man He made into woman, and He brought her to the man." Gen. 2:21-22(NKJV)

"Therefore, a man shall leave his father and mother and be joined to his wife, and they shall become one flesh." Gen. 2:24(NKJV).

"One flesh" defines the unity God intends in the relationship between a man and his wife. The intimacy intended within this relationship is not just physical intimacy. It is an intimacy of the entire person, body, soul, and spirit. An intimacy that will continue to grow throughout their lives.

When God says "I will make a helper comparable to him," He affirms the equality of both the husband and his wife. God did not take from the head or the foot of man, but He took man's rib. The picture is a helper equal to man, alongside him, close to his heart.

God is a god of order. The family, which is the foundation of our social structure, is intended to be a reflection of the very nature of God Himself. Within the Trinity, there are distinct roles. Although the Father, Son, and Holy Spirit are each one fully God and therefore equal, they have different roles. There is also a clear line of authority. 1 John 4:9-11(ESV), "In this, the love of God was made manifest among us, that God sent his only Son into the world so that we might live through him. In this is love, not that we have loved God but that he loved us and sent his Son to be the propitiation for our sins." The Lord Jesus came to earth in total submission to God the Father.

Husbands are commanded to love their wives, and wives are commanded to submit to their husbands. These commands are often incorrectly taken to reflect inequality. We tend to think of submission in negative terms but we should not, for Jesus' response in submitting Himself to the Father was in every sense a very positive thing. Just as wives are commanded to be submissive to their own husbands, if the husband is fulfilling his responsibility to love his wife as Christ loves the church, her offer should be a natural response. As followers of Christ, we are expected to submit to Him trusting that everything that He desires for us is for His glory and works together for our own good.

If asked what he envisions by the term "helper", most men, whether they readily admit it or not, would reply, "Someone to pick up my dirty laundry, wash and iron it, prepare my meals, meet my sexual needs, and bear me children." That is probably what I would have said.

Ann and I had the perfect marriage, Ann came willing to give everything and I came willing to take it all. From the moment I said, "I do", I began to systematically destroy the love that she brought to the marriage. Not by intent, certainly, but just because of my own self-centeredness. If I had been asked if I loved Ann, I would have said yes, but I don't believe anyone has the capacity to truly understand love until they begin to understand God's love for them.

I now realize that I had what psychiatrists would define as a fear of intimacy. Everything I had learned as a young man emphasized the need to be independent and self-sufficient. I could give up to a point, but I was unable to allow myself to become emotionally dependent. Fear of rejection caused me to push away. Such an attitude may help one as a fighter pilot, but it certainly doesn't help a man as a husband, father, or his role in other close interpersonal relationships. When I felt myself being drawn too close emotionally, I felt as though I were being smothered or suffocated, and the natural response was to push away. In my relationship with Ann, that was accomplished with a verbal stiff arm.

I viewed marriage as a fifty-fifty proposition. Picture a football field. I could go as far as the fifty-yard line and no further. One serious problem with such a view is that no two people would define the fifty-yard line the same.

When I surrendered my life to Christ, whatever happened to me personally was no longer my responsibility. If I gave completely and unconditionally, and as a result experienced the hurt and the pain of rejection, that was His responsibility. I no longer needed to strive to protect myself. The fifty-yard line no longer existed. I knew God wanted me to love my wife without reservation, so it was up to me to learn how to do that and simply trust Him with the outcome.

Ephesians 5:25(NKJV) says, "Husbands, love your wives just as Christ also loved the church and gave Himself for her." Most men would agree that this means to love her unconditionally, but it means so much more. It means to love her so that she can perceive that love. How do I know that God loves me? All I need to do to know God loves me is to look at Calvary. Scripture says, "but God shows his love for us in that while we were still sinners, Christ died for us." Romans5:8 (ESV) God communicated His love to me in a way that I could see and understand. If my wife is to know that I love her, I must learn to express it in a way that she can see, understand, and accept.

I know, from the verses in I John 5:11-15, there is nothing I can do that will jeopardize God's love for me, because my eternal security is not based on my performance. So, if I am going to love my wife as God loves the church, my wife needs to know that there is nothing she can do to stop me from loving her. God will never leave me nor forsake me, and Ann needs to know that I will never leave her nor forsake her.

Scripture also tells me that God always listens. I can pray at any time or in any place and know that God is ready to listen. Once again, if I am to love Ann as God loves the church, I need to learn how to apply this principle to our communication. This has not been easy for me, but it is something that I know I need to do. Hopefully, I've made some progress and, although I'll never do it perfectly, I intend to continue to learn to be a better listener and a better communicator as well.

I was really challenged one morning by a Christian friend who said, "If we are to love our wives as Christ loves the church, then every promise that God makes to us as believers is a promise that we, in turn, should be able to make to our wives." That really blew me away. That meant that learning to love my wife was going to be a life-long challenge.

I know that I will never love Ann perfectly, and I also know that I can never love Ann as God desires, in my own strength. I do know that I can only love her as God intends as I allow Him to do it through me, by the power of the Holy Spirit. That means I am totally dependent on Him.

In addressing the issue of your wife as a helper, I don't mean to suggest that God is not interested in whether your laundry needs, dietary needs, and sexual needs are met or not. However, I believe that He is much more interested in your personal relationship with Him. God is in the process of conforming me to the image of His Son. No one is used by God more than my wife in accomplishing His purpose. My relationship with Ann is the clearest measure of my willingness to surrender my will to Him. I can fool the guys at work, the neighbors, and the folks at church, but if you really want to know how I am doing spiritually, ask my wife or observe how I treat her and how willing I am to seek to serve her and her needs. If I am seeking to love her as I should, I should not be doing it for her response but out of obedience to God. If I am loving her in hopes that she will, in turn, meet my needs, it is no longer unconditional and can only be described as manipulation. I don't care how bad one considers his marriage, if he can see the significance of his spouse in helping him to grow in his personal relationship with Christ, he will thank God and appreciate the mate God has given him.

If I were to love my wife as God intended, very simply, I needed to act in love no matter what emotions I might be feeling at any given moment.

David DeWitt says in his book, *The Mature Man*, "Romance is a boy thing but love is a man thing." An interesting note is that the more I acted in love, the more I fell in love with Ann. My son, Will, asked me several years ago, "Is Christianity just pie in the sky?"

At the time, I was mentoring two men: one was in his third marriage and the other was going through his third divorce. I told my son, "No, it is not pie in the sky. I am absolutely head over heels in love with your mom. That, my son, is a God thing."

# CHAPTER 6

# *Flight Crew*

## *Teamwork*

I am so thankful for the men who initially came alongside me when I surrendered my life to Christ. These men gave me the encouragement and accountability I needed to get established in my new-found faith.

One year after my initial commitment, my friend, Hank McGrew, told me about a family conference that was held each summer at Covenant College on Lookout Mountain. I had been looking for a place to take my family, where we would have the opportunity to grow in our Christian faith, and this seemed to fit the bill. It was here that I was first introduced to CBMC and met men whose hearts beat in sync with mine. They were men, from different denominations, who had all come into a personal relationship with Jesus Christ and were committed to helping other men discover who Jesus was, and how what he had done applied to them. It was a wonderful week for each of us, and this would become an annual affair for us for many years.

The ministry of CBMC consisted of teams of men, called committees, in cities throughout the country. These committees would gather weekly for men to share their challenges and successes, have a short devotional, and pray for other men by name. The emphasis of their prayer was for relatives, friends, and acquaintances to come to a saving knowledge of Christ.

Upon returning to Covington from that first family conference, I called several other men and together we organized a local committee. In praying for others, we used what we called our "ten most wanted" list. Each man listed the ten people that he most wanted to see come to Christ. This list became a reminder to pray for them daily. My mother, father, two brothers, and my sister were at the top of my list. I prayed for the older of my two brothers, Charlie, for five years before he came to Christ. Michael, the younger, surrendered his life to Christ three years after that and my sister, Jean, came to a saving knowledge after thirty-two years. I challenged my mother to read through the Bible in a year, and after reading through two years straight, at the age of seventy, she pushed her cocktail glass away and began to grow in her faith. My parents attended a CBMC outreach event, and after hearing a man to whom he could relate sharing his personal story, my dad professed faith in Christ.

In addition to the weekly prayer sessions, CBMC committees held periodic outreach meetings in the form of luncheons, dinners, or leadership and governmental prayer breakfasts, where a guest speaker was invited to share his own story of coming to faith. The entire event was designed to reach uncommitted men and women with an intelligent presentation of who Jesus Christ is and what He had done for them. Guests were usually followed up with a visit and given an opportunity to make a personal commitment.

CBMC became a major part of my life and gave me opportunities to share my faith, both as a participant in inviting others, and as an outreach speaker. Mature Christian men also gave me the written materials and training that I needed to disciple and help other men grow in their Christian faith. I am so thankful for the opportunities afforded me and the encouragement and accountability I was able to experience through the men of CBMC.

In the late nineties, the ministry was going through a crisis, and following my retirement from Delta, I was able to step up and provide leadership as President of CBMC. I am a strong proponent of team leadership and, with a team of godly men, we were able to return the ministry to financial viability, reexamine the ministry's core values, and present a fresh vision statement. Those core values are a reflection of my own ministry core values:

(1) The Preeminence of Christ: Intimacy with Christ is paramount, and all that we do must emanate from our life in Christ and His life in ours.
(2) Life-on-Life Relationships: We value the process of one-on-one relationships for evangelism and discipleship.
(3) Teams: God calls us to work together in teams in order to multiply what He wants to accomplish through us.
(4) Generational Spiritual Reproduction: The goal of the discipleship process is spiritual reproduction to the 3rd and 4th generations and beyond.

**The CBMC Vision:**
**For all Men in our Movement to Experience**
**The Power of One God**
**The Value of One Man**
**The Leverage of One Team**
**Resulting in Spiritual Reproduction among**
**Businessmen throughout the World**

From my earliest participation in sports, I was exposed to and learned the value of teamwork. This was reinforced throughout my time at the Naval Academy and subsequent naval flight training. Formation flying is all a matter of teamwork, and the Navy's F-4 was designed for one pilot working with a radar intercept officer or RIO in the backseat. Flying combat in Vietnam proved over and over the value of the pilot and RIO coordinating and executing their appropriate roles. All of this emphasis on teamwork carried over to airline flying, and resource management training became a major part of airline training. Since teamwork in the cockpit was emphasized and evaluated in pilot proficiency evaluation checks, as a Senior Flight Instructor, I was able to observe teamwork first hand.

The most basic team for a married man is the man and his wife. Had it not been for the support of my wife, there is no way I could have fulfilled my responsibilities as a husband, father, and airline pilot, and still have had time for meaningful ministry. Ann is my greatest supporter, but she can also be my harshest critic. I appreciate her criticism as well as her praise, and even though I can get defensive when I feel that her criticism is unwarranted, I have learned that there is almost always a degree of truth in what she has said. I believe the most dangerous leader is one who surrounds himself with "yes" men. I appreciate those on my team who are bold enough to challenge me. Although I may not agree with them, at least they have given me a reason to thoroughly think through my decision and pray about it. As an airline captain, I would always begin my brief with the co-pilot by telling him: "Never assume I know what I am doing. If you question anything I'm doing speak up. I will not get my feelings hurt. If I am right, we haven't lost a thing. If I happen to be wrong, you have saved us some embarrassment and maybe a whole lot more."

When speaking with others about the value of a team, I tell men, "Look at the man on your right. I don't know what your IQ is, but I guarantee that the IQ of you and the man on your right is greater than yours alone. Now, look at the man on your left. I don't know what your spiritual giftedness is, but I guarantee that the spiritual giftedness of you and the man on your left is greater than yours alone."

In order to meet the challenges that all men face, we need other men. Thankfully, I have always been able to find a small group of men who are willing to listen, to pray for me, and to hold me accountable.

# CHAPTER 7

# *Managing Fuel*
## *Stewardship*

When I decided to leave the military, I really didn't know what to do with my life. I had been drawn to the military as a career because I loved my country and thought that a military career would fulfill the need to live a meaningful, purposeful life. I believe that many young men are drawn to the military for the very same reason. This was certainly the case following 9/11. However, combat has a way of turning idealism to cynicism, and so many young men struggle when their service is complete, because of the subsequent loss of purpose. This lack of meaning exacerbates the post-traumatic stress disorder they may already struggle with due to the trauma of combat itself.

I left the military with two primary goals. The first was to see how much money I could make. The second was to eventually get involved in politics and see if I couldn't help change the world, making it a better place for my children and my grandchildren. In light of the first goal, which I somehow felt would be a measure of my success, I looked for every way I could to make a buck. I am and always have been fiscally conservative, and even before becoming a Christian, I believed that one should live within his means and avoid unnecessary debt. When I began to read the Bible, I discovered that this was clearly a biblical principle. Scripture states that "The rich rule over the poor, and the borrower is a slave to the lender." Proverbs 22:7(NIV).

Working with CBMC and other men to reach our community with the claims of Christ, we looked for creative ways to introduce businessmen to biblical principles. Learning of a man in Atlanta who was beginning a ministry based on finance, I contacted Larry Burkett and invited him to come to Covington, Louisiana, for a weekend seminar. We rented the community center and mailed out invitations to the entire community of accountants, financial planners, and anyone associated with money management, inviting them to a seminar on Friday night and Saturday. Each one who attended received a notebook on managing their money. The seminar was a huge success, establishing our credibility in the area, and facilitating future outreach efforts, as well as introducing men and women to all the Bible has to say about money.

Larry Burkett's material, "Managing Your Money", went on to become a major ministry. Of all the many lives in Covington that were impacted by Larry's material, I believe that I benefited the most. I learned that the Bible has more to say about money than about any other single subject. The book of Proverbs became my guide for managing my own finances.

It was about this same time that I was approached by another pilot who asked me to invest in a water processor designed to distill drinking water. It appeared to be a sure bet. Considering that most of the drinking water for the city of New Orleans comes from the Mississippi River, how could such an investment fail? In the Delta pilots' lounge at Lambert Field in St. Louis, there used to be a sign over the urinal in the men's room which read, "Please flush. New Orleans needs the drinking water."

I had given a verbal commitment to the pilot who was spearheading the investment. The only problem was that my commitment was going to require me to co-sign a note. Reading what the book of Proverbs said about co-signing a note, I knew that if I proceeded with my commitment, I would be clearly violating a biblical principle. After prayer and careful consideration, I went to the pilot and asked him to release me from my obligation. I told him I had become a Christian, and because of what the Bible said, I did not feel I could proceed further. He didn't understand, but nonetheless graciously released me from my charge. The project ended up a complete failure, and several other pilots lost their entire investments. A number of years later, I was pleased to hear that the pilot who headed up the investment had come to Christ.

Before I came to Christ, there was a time when I thought that perhaps material wealth and possessions would satisfy and fill that void in my life. I expected one day to own a boat, an airplane of my own, and some investment properties. When we moved to Covington, on the north shore of Lake Ponchartrain, I felt we were well on the way. I had begun to earn a decent salary with the airline, we had built a new home, had two new automobiles, and I had opened a Swiss bank account, speculating in silver bullion. However, it soon became apparent, as I looked at senior pilots and other people around me who already owned the material things I desired, that the ownership of these things would not guarantee happiness and satisfy the longing for whatever was missing in my life.

The scripture verse that became and remains a favorite of mine to this day is Matthew 6:33(NKJV) where Jesus said, "But seek first the kingdom of God and His righteousness and all these things shall be added to you." In context, Jesus is telling us that we cannot serve two masters; we cannot serve God and riches. He goes on to say that we need not worry about food and clothing, for God knows and will supply our needs. I can honestly say that the things I had desired before were no longer important and I no longer pursued them. What is fascinating to me is that, although I no longer sought them, I have, for one reason or another, experienced the ownership of almost every one of those things.

When our son asked if Christianity was pie-in-the sky, I explained that the depth of my love for his mother was a "God thing". It is true that I have always loved her, but my capacity to love increased tremendously when I came to the realization of how much God loved me. The second thing I said to him concerned finances. One of the two pilots I was discipling owed fifty thousand dollars on a credit card which he was unable to pay, and the other had to trade in his Honda automobile because he could no longer afford the payments. Both of them were well senior to me on the airline and had been earning much more than I had as an airline captain. On the other hand, we owned our home and had no debts. That was, once again, a "God thing" because we had chosen to follow God's principles in the handling of our finances.

2004 was a challenging year. This was approximately seven years after my retirement from Delta. Delta Airlines declared bankruptcy, dissolving the pilot pension fund, and as a result, I lost three-fourths of my retirement annuity and our health insurance. Hurricane Ivan struck Pensacola, causing us out-of-pocket uninsurable losses of $75,000. In addition, during the same three-month period, I discovered that I had been defrauded by the financial manager of my IRA. He had stolen $100,000 from my IRA investment account. Had we not been following biblical principles, we would have been devastated, but instead of financial ruin, we simply couldn't give as much to ministries and charitable organizations as we had before. We also needed to be more careful in managing our remaining assets.

There is great freedom in being out of debt. We live in a materialistic culture where charge cards and credit card debt are a way of life. I do use a credit card, but only for the purpose of record keeping. My monthly credit card statement allows me to easily keep a record of my spending habits, and provides the information I need for completing my tax forms. I pay off my credit card bill every month and have never allowed it to carry over from one month to another. Remaining debt free allows one to follow whatever direction God might lead.

Being debt free also allows one freedom in pursuing vocational choices. Some people have been precluded from going into full-time ministry simply because they were in debt. Following my retirement from Delta, CBMC, the ministry with which I had been associated for so many years, was going through a major crisis. There was not only a crisis of leadership, but also a financial crisis. At the height of the financial situation, the ministry was over three million dollars in debt. I felt that God was clearly calling me to step forward to fill the leadership vacuum, so when the opportunity presented itself, because I was debt free, I was able to take the position of president of the organization without pay. A salary was offered, but since I didn't need the money, the salary was refused. We began to apply the same biblical principles to the ministry that I had applied in the management of my personal finances, and the ministry was soon out of debt.

I used to believe that I owned the material things that I purchased or possessed. I came to realize that I don't own anything; God owns it all. He simply allows me the use of these things and my role is that of a steward. Again, there is great freedom in recognizing that God owns it. It is senseless to worry about losing what I may possess but don't own. He does hold me accountable as a steward, however, so it behooves me to ensure that I make the best use of what He entrusts to my care.

# CHAPTER 8

# *Flying Through Turbulence*
## *Suffering*

"If it were any better, I couldn't stand it." Have you ever heard those words? I can't relate, because that just isn't my experience. I use the term "plastic Christians" for those who always say that things couldn't be better.

When I speak publicly and offer people an opportunity to make a commitment of faith, I clearly tell them that if they make such a decision, it doesn't mean their life will be a "bed of roses". In fact, I tell them quite the opposite. I have known the hardest times in my life since that point in time, and it has certainly been harder than flying combat over North Vietnam. I have, however, had certain stability in my life and there is no other way I could have had that stability.

As I consider the high suicide rate of veterans today, I think of my own friends who lost their lives after returning from Vietnam. No, they didn't commit suicide directly, but was it indirect? Paul said in Ephesians 2:12(NIV), "Remember that at that time you were separate from Christ, excluded from citizenship in Israel and foreigners to the covenants of the promise, without hope and without God in the world." Those words: "having no hope and without God," are to me the saddest words in all of Scripture. They are words of desperation. What saved me from the destructive pattern of behavior associated with PTSD after Vietnam was surrendering my life completely to Christ. It didn't save me from PTSD, but it did save me from myself.

When life deals us things that are difficult or when we go through times of suffering, we are inclined to ask, "God, why are you doing this? Why is this happening to me?" These times of suffering can be related to any number of issues. Health, relationships, financial pressures, and career pressures are just a few. Men have a way of looking good on the outside, when in reality, life is bursting at the seams on the inside.

For the first eight and a half years after coming to Christ, I felt like I was riding the crest of a wave of successes. Then in an instant, my life was suddenly falling apart. In my marriage, I had sown seeds of emotional pain. It wasn't my intent, but just through my own self-centeredness. Ann had built a wall around her emotions to protect herself from me. When Ann asked me a direct question about an issue in the past and I gave her an honest answer, that wall began to crack. All of the anger that she had stuffed after my return from Vietnam began to spew forth. It was like a volcano erupting. Now I lived with someone who absolutely hated me. It is true that I was learning to be the husband that God intended for me to be from the beginning, but the history of my life before Christ remained. Although I was forgiven for the pain that I had caused my wife, repentance does not take away the consequences of our choices or actions.

When we experience times of suffering from a human perspective, we might be inclined to say God doesn't know, God doesn't care, or God just can't do anything about it. These are all arguments that people have used against Christianity. There is a fourth option, and that is what one of my friends chose to do after spending seven and a half years as a POW in North Vietnam. He has chosen to deny reason and say there is no God. He refuses to believe in a God who would allow him to go through so much pain. When someone tells me that he is an atheist, my question, which is rhetorical, is: "Is that an intellectual decision or an emotional decision?"

Scriptures do not come right out and tell us why, but they do tell us we are called to suffer. That isn't something we like to hear. They also tell us there is purpose in what we experience. Knowing there is purpose can provide comfort in the midst of our suffering. Philippians1:29(ESV): "For it has been granted to you that for the sake of Christ you should not only believe in him but also suffer for his sake."

Galatians 2:20(ESV) says "I have been crucified with Christ. It is no longer I who live, but Christ who lives in me. And the life I now live in the flesh I live by faith in the Son of God, who loved me and gave himself for me." When I was baptized, my baptism was an outward expression of my identification with Jesus's death, burial, and resurrection. If this is true, should I not also suffer with Christ?

Was my experience for no apparent reason? The pain of my failure to live up to my own standards is what brought me to the end of myself and led me in desperation to cry out to God in the first place. The suffering I experienced as my family fell apart stripped me of my pride. "God resists the proud but gives grace to the humble." James 4:6(NKJV) This was a time of testing of my faith. Was I going to seek to meet my own needs or trust God to meet those needs? Through my pain, I grew in my intimacy with Christ and learned to persevere. Romans 5:3(ESV); "Not only that, but we rejoice in our sufferings, knowing that suffering produces endurance." The testing of our faith produces character.

Oswald Chambers in *My Utmost for His Highest* writes: "In the Bible, clouds are always associated with God. Clouds are the sorrows, sufferings, or providential circumstances, within or without our personal lives, which actually seem to contradict the sovereignty of God. Yet it is through these very clouds that the Spirit of God is teaching us how to walk by faith. If there were never any clouds in our lives, we would have no faith. 'The clouds are the dust of His feet.' Nahum 1:3(ESV). They are a sign that God is there. What a revelation it is to know that sorrow, bereavement, and suffering are actually the clouds that come along with God! God cannot come near us without clouds, He does not come in clear-shining brightness."

Suffering for no apparent reason can cause great frustration. It can seem so indiscriminate. Why does a tornado destroy one house and not the one next door? It is difficult to understand, but we must remember, we are fallen men in a fallen world. God's entire order was impacted by man's rebellion.

Walt Hendrichsen writes in *Thoughts from the Diary of a Desperate Man*: "We want to be convinced that something is good by either personal experience, our sense of justice or reasoning that the end justifies the means. Providence can call into question God's goodness but we must never try to discern God's goodness by personal experience. God's goodness is something the believer affirms by faith rather than experience. We must acknowledge that we were created for His good pleasure…. Much of what you observe and experience seems to suggest a callous indifference to what we would normally call good."

The suffering in my own life has deepened my yearning for my life to come. About six months after I had retired from

Delta Airlines, Ann said, "You're depressed." Men tend to keep depression at bay through hyperactivity, and I no longer had the activity of my job as an airline captain.

"I know I'm depressed", I responded, "but I think I'm handling it pretty well."

"You're not handling it as well as you think you are." At her insistence, as well as the encouragement of our daughter Karen, I made an appointment to see a psychiatrist in Atlanta.

During the course of the appointment, he asked: "How do you feel about death?"

"I'm looking forward to it," I responded.

He didn't particularly like my answer, but how could I, as a Christ follower, not be looking forward to being in His very presence? If I believe God's Word, I have a future with my Heavenly Father that is beyond my comprehension.

Romans 8:18-22(ESV) says, "For I consider that the sufferings of this present time are not worth comparing with the glory that is to be revealed to us. For the creation waits with eager longing for the revealing of the sons of God. For the creation was subjected to futility, not willingly, but because of him who subjected it, in hope that the creation itself will be set free from its bondage to corruption and obtain the freedom of the glory of the children of God. For we know that the whole creation has been groaning together in the pains of childbirth until now." The sufferings that I experience during this life deepen my yearning for the life to come.

When we go through periods of suffering, instead of just asking, "Why is this happening to me?", we should seek to find God in the midst of it. If purpose can be found in the pain, we can also find God's comfort.

When our nine-month-old grandson, Noah, tragically

drowned in his family's swimming pool, we were all devastated. It occurred on a beautiful afternoon in August. Our son-in-law had just arrived at his job as an emergency room physician when the call came in of a drowning incident, and the ambulance returned with his own son. Unable to resuscitate him, Noah was placed on life support. At the first opportunity, Noah's dad, Andrew, brought our daughter Denise and the other five children together, and in the midst of his pain assured them that God was not asleep and had not made a mistake. He was to spend the next thirty days at the hospital, either at Noah's bedside, working in the emergency room, or at his computer sending out prayer requests. His messages were those of a grieving father torn between his love for God and his love for his son.

During the time that Noah was on life support, our daughter Denise never left the hospital floor. Ann took over the responsibility of caring for the other five children and I shuttled between the hospital and home. The drowning had occurred on a Saturday, but it would be the following Friday before the cranial swelling would subside enough to check for brain activity. As the week progressed my hope soared. I spent much time in prayer, and we received telephone and e-mail messages from people who were praying from as far as Johannesburg, South Africa, and Seoul, Korea. I went from no hope to a belief that God would heal Noah. You cannot imagine my disappointment when on Friday the tests showed little, if any, chance of recovery. I spent my night crying and railing at God for missing such an opportunity to show Himself strong.

The next morning at the hospital, I found Denise perfectly calm and at peace. She told me about a visitor who asked if she could go in and pray for Noah, who was in intensive care. After Denise gave her permission, the stranger soon reappeared, saying that she had prayed for Noah, and believed that he would recover and have a great ministry. "He is having a great ministry", Denise replied. "Dad, why do people believe that he must recover to have a great ministry? People everywhere are hearing about Noah and going to God in prayer. Noah is touching hearts because, in his innocence, he is like a drop of a very fine perfume. If he were to live, he would be tainted by sin and although he could impact lives, he would be more like a body splash."

Romans 8:28(NKJV), "And we know that all things work together for good for those who love God, to those who are called according to His purpose." I continued to grieve, yes, but because I found God's purpose through the words of my daughter, I was able to find comfort in the midst of my suffering.

Scripture says: "Give thanks in all circumstances; for this is God's will for you in Christ Jesus." 1 Thessalonians 5:18(NIV). Knowing that I was commanded to give thanks in all circumstances was one thing, but to really mean it was something else.

"I'm in real pain Lord. I can say thank you but you know I don't really mean it. Please help me." I wrestled with this for a long time and really could find no answers until one day as I was reading through the book of Hebrews, I read: "And without faith it is impossible to please God, because anyone who comes to Him must believe that He exists and that He rewards those who earnestly seek Him." Hebrews 1:6(NIV)

How much faith does it really take to go through each day when everything is going my way? Do I really believe that without faith it's impossible to please God? If I really believe this, then, when I find myself in a situation that I can deal with only by faith, rather than an obstacle, it is an opportunity. It's an opportunity to please God. Knowing that He has given me such an opportunity, I can now give thanks and really mean it.

# CHAPTER 9

# *Final Approach*
## *Leaving a Legacy*

Not only has God given me the ability to learn how to love my wife unconditionally, but He gave me the ability to learn to love my three beautiful children as well. I was very performance oriented, and unfortunately, my children grew up under the same performance-based paradigm. It has taken many years to try to break that paradigm, but I can now say, because each of my children has at one time or another broken my heart, they are learning that I love them unconditionally. I believe that they all either know or at least have reason to believe that I will love them no matter what.

When Ann learned that she was pregnant with our first child, the thought of being a father gave me a tremendous sense of responsibility. I believe that it was that sense of responsibility that motivated me to study as hard as I did in advanced flight training ground school.

Ann and I both wanted to be good parents, so we read everything we could on parenting. At the time Dr. Spock was considered the foremost authority on parenting. We questioned his methods and reasoning, and I remember reading and wondering if I had ruined my children's creativity or destroyed their self-confidence. Ann was a great mother, but I felt very unsure in my role as a father.

When I surrendered my life to Christ, I was so thankful that my children were as young as they were. I believed that I could now teach them biblical principles and they would avoid all of the mistakes I had made. Well, it is true that I could teach those principles that would lead them to a personal relationship with Christ, but I could not live their lives for them. It took me a long time to learn and understand that I am driven by the desire to control, and no matter how much I might want to control others, control is an illusion. God alone is ultimately in control. The only one I am responsible for trying to control is myself.

Ann and I had always been concerned with providing the best education we possibly could for our children. With this in mind, we sought the best schools we could find. Even though we supplemented church with devotions at home, we soon realized that we were sending our children off five days each week, for seven hours, to an institution that held an entirely different worldview. If all the resources that are available today for homeschooling had been available then, we probably would have chosen to home school. Since they were not, God placed on our hearts the vision for a Christian school.

As we began praying, I shared my vision with the one man I knew who was familiar with Christian education. Stuart McClendon, an attorney, had a child who had attended Ben Lippen School in Asheville, North Carolina. Stuart joined me in prayer, and I invited a Christian school administrator from Indianapolis, Indiana to visit Covington, Louisiana and talk about Christian education. As a result of several home meetings, three additional men surfaced, who cared enough to get involved. The five of us met one night in April and decided that we would trust God to provide so we could open a Christian school, kindergarten through high school, the next September. Since the men thought that airline pilots had more free time than anyone else, I was elected chairman of the founding board. We had no buildings, no curriculum, no teachers, no students, and no money. What we did have, however, was a God-given vision, and faith in a God who is able to do the impossible

Our entire family was fully involved, and the next September Northlake Christian School opened the school year with 110 students. At the start of the second year, there were 170 students, and by the third year, the school had 210 students and sixteen acres for a permanent school site. At no time during those first three years did the school incur any debt.

There was a time when I would stand with my family and quote Joshua, "But if serving the LORD seems undesirable to you, then choose for yourselves this day whom you will serve, whether the gods your ancestors served beyond the Euphrates, or the gods of the Amorites, in whose land you are living. But as for me and my household, we will serve the LORD." Joshua 24:15(NIV).

I was so puffed up with pride. As God took me through the process of stripping away that pride, I realized I had held such tight control, that my family members didn't have the freedom to seek their own way. I now know I can control no one other than myself. I learned that I am not to try to be the Holy Spirit in the lives of my children or my wife. That is God's role. What I can do is set an example and earnestly and consistently pray for them.

If you were to ask me where I best learned principles of leadership, I would tell you in the home. I didn't learn them in leadership classes at the Naval Academy, or in cockpit management seminars on the airline. I learned the principles of leadership that I adhere to today as a husband and a father.

I am convinced that the role of a leader is simply to help create an environment where others can grow to their greatest potential before God. The conductor doesn't try to play the instrument of each member of the orchestra. He assists them by directing in such a way that the individual members can give their maximum performance.

As a new Christian, I discovered that the Bible gave principles on raising children and teaching them values that other books did not provide. I gained the confidence that as I tried to apply these principles, I would be doing for my children the best that I could. I am not saying that I always got it right, for I certainly did not. I took Proverbs 13:24(NIV) literally: "Whoever spares the rod hates their children, but the one who loves their children is careful to discipline them." I did use the paddle or switch when I deemed it appropriate.

Each of my children responded differently. Denise did need an occasional spanking, to which she was very responsive. Karen was very compliant and rarely needed a paddling. The one regret I have is the way I disciplined Will. What I thought was passive-aggressive behavior was, in fact, attention deficit disorder. Will was in college before I understood what he was trying to deal with because of his ADD. I grieve over the spankings given for what I thought was rebellion. I have asked for his forgiveness and even though I am forgiven, I still grieve. I will say I should have known better. If a certain kind of discipline is not accomplishing its intended result, don't continue to use it. All children are different. Find what works for each individual child.

Someone once suggested that when the child does something which justifies a spanking, in order to show them what Jesus did for us by taking the punishment for our sins, we should take the spanking and make them administer the punishment. That sounded reasonable, so I decided to give it a try. The next time Denise deserved a spanking, I handed her the paddle and bent over so she could deliver the blows. She was absolutely traumatized. It was evident that she would have much rather taken the punishment herself. I made her go ahead and administer the spanking. When it came time for Will to receive a spanking, it was quite different. He thought this was a great idea and really let me have it. I could readily see that this wasn't as good an idea as I had originally thought.

Parenting is perhaps the hardest thing I have ever done. At times it has also appeared to be the most unrewarding thing I've done. Each of my children has, at one time or another, disappointed me. I can only imagine how I have at times grieved my Heavenly Father with my own behavior. Nevertheless, I cannot imagine life without the three of them. I now ache as I see them experience the same heartbreaks with their own children. I want so badly to heal their hurts, but understand that their Heavenly Father loves them even more than I do. Since each of my children has decided to follow Christ, I take comfort in knowing that: "All things work together for good to those who love God, to those who are called according to his purpose." Romans 8:28(NKJV).

The most important thing I can do for my children is to pray for them and their children as our sovereign Lord goes about the process of conforming them to the image of His Son. With my desire to fix things, I must ensure that I don't get in His way.

If I were to leave my children with all of the material possessions in the world, I will have left them with nothing. However, if I can leave them with an abiding faith in the Lord Jesus, I will have left them with everything.

When I am gone, I want each of my children to be able to say two things about me. First, I want them to be able to say, "Daddy really loved God." They will not be able to say this on the basis of what I say, but on the basis of how they see me live my life. My priorities and actions are what will define my love. Secondly, I want them each to be able to say, "Dad really loved me." If they can say that, once again, it won't be on the basis of what I say. It will be on the basis of how I have lived my life.

# APPENDIX

As long as we still draw breath, it is never too late to help another. For the uncommitted, it has been my desire to share the hope that I have, and ensure that others understand how much God loves them and know what He has done for them personally. I believe that if I were the only person on planet Earth, Jesus loves me so much that He would have died for me. I believe that same truth for everyone.

"On the Fritz" is simply a compilation of messages written over a period of time, designed to challenge others to think about things of eternal value. Each message was prayerfully written to deepen the faith of those who do have a personal relationship with our living God, and perhaps awaken those who have no relationship.

The messages were written to be contained on a single e-mail page, and recipients were encouraged to forward them on or use them in whatever way they deemed appropriate.

# ON THE FRITZ

## *"A Drop of Fine Perfume"*

During the time that my grandson, Noah, was on life support, my daughter Denise never left the hospital floor. Noah's father, Andrew, never left the hospital, spending his time either in the emergency room as an emergency room physician or in Noah's room. Ann took over the responsibility of caring for the other five children and I shuttled between the hospital and home. The drowning had occurred on a Saturday, but it would be the following Friday before the swelling would subside enough to check for brain activity. As the week progressed, my hope soared. I spent much time in prayer, and we received telephone and e-mail messages from people who were praying from as far a Johannesburg, South Africa, and Seoul, Korea. I went from no hope to believe that God would heal him. You cannot imagine my disappointment when on Friday the tests showed little if any chance of recovery. I spent my night crying and railing at God for missing such an opportunity to show Himself strong.

The next morning at the hospital, 1 found Denise perfectly calm and at peace. She told me about a visitor who asked if she could go in and pray for Noah who was in intensive care. After giving her permission, the stranger soon reappeared saying that she had prayed for Noah and believed that he would recover and have a great ministry. "He is having a great ministry", Denise replied.

"Dad, why do people believe he must recover to have a great ministry? People everywhere are hearing about Noah and going to God in prayer. Noah is touching hearts because, in his innocence, he is like a drop of a fine perfume. If he were to live, he would be tainted by sin, and although he could impact lives, he would be more like a body splash." Romans 8:28(NKJV) "And we know that all things work together for good for those who love God, to those who are called according to His purpose."

Noah did not recover, but I had the opportunity to hold him once more, and after thirty days, he was taken off life support. Denise soon got pregnant again and had another son named Josiah, which in Hebrew means "the God that heals." Two years later, Josiah's brother Owen was born. God gave Denise and Andrew two for the one He took.

If I were to leave my children material wealth without faith based on truth, I would leave them nothing. If, on the other hand, I leave them a strong faith based on truth, I leave them everything they need for this life and the hope for the life to come.

So, what will your children's inheritance be? Will it help them survive life's tragedies?

# "God Has Nothing to do With Politics"

The decision to resign my commission was not a difficult one. Angered by our nation's no-win policy, the rules of engagement, and the way the war was being micromanaged from the White House, I felt that I had no choice. To resign was the only honorable way I could protest. Although my decision wasn't difficult, it was traumatic. You see, I do believe the military is an honorable profession, and all I had ever wanted to do was to make it my career. Receiving the letter that my resignation would be tentatively accepted one year from the date it was submitted, I began to think, what am I going to do with the rest of my life?

Money had never been important to me, but I determined if I can't be an Admiral, I will see how much money I can make and eventually get involved in politics. I had two small children and it didn't take much to conclude that if our country kept going in the direction we were headed, soon it wouldn't be a suitable place for my children or my grandchildren. With this in mind, I got involved in grassroots politics and began to see if I could help make this world a better place in which to live. I believed if we could just get the right man elected, we could get the whole mess turned around and moving in the right direction. However, we never seemed to get the right man elected. I finally concluded that even if we did, those men were unable to solve those problems in their own strength. I further concluded I was unable to be the father or the husband I wanted to be. No matter how hard I might try, in my own strength, I just could not be the person I had determined to be. Confronted with biblical truth, and coming to grips with my own depravity, I decided if I could know God, I wanted to know Him, and I was willing to meet Him on His terms. I came out of the cave with my hands up. The change was profound, and I soon had a new list of priorities.

In spite of the changes, I can still get very emotional about politics. Please don't misunderstand me; I appreciate people who are community conscious. However, I believe the only way we are really going to have a changed world is to have changed men, and the only one who can change a man is Jesus Christ. The Bible says "Therefore, if anyone is in Christ, he is a new creation." 2 Corinthians 5:17(NKJV)

A recent political e-mail sent by my wife to her nephew solicited the response, "God has nothing to do with politics." Quite the contrary, "He changes the times and the seasons; He removes kings and raises up kings; He gives wisdom to the wise and knowledge to those who have understanding." Daniel 2:21(NKJV). God is interested in all that we do, and I believe that it is my responsibility to vote for and support godly candidates.

Have you decided who you will vote for? On what basis have you made your decision?

ON THE FRITZ

# *"Which Way is Up"*

"It's time to raise the hood." I was just beginning the instrument phase of my basic flight training in the T-2 Buckeye at Meridian NAS, and the purpose of the hood was to block all visual references outside of the cockpit. The instructor turned onto the runway and initiated our takeoff. Once airborne, on his command, I began slow turns first right and then left.

Man's equilibrium is dependent on three basic inputs. First, he has the visual cue to those things around him. Secondly, he has the gravitational pull on the joints of the body. Thirdly, he has fluid in the semi-circular canal of the inner ear. The movement of this fluid is sensed by little hairs that send a signal to the brain that the body is in motion.

Now as long as none of these inputs are impeded, the aviator is in pretty good shape. But what happens if he loses one? Say, for instance, he flies into a cloud bank, or as in my particular instance, he puts up the instrument hood. He has now lost the visual cue to those things around him. Let's then say he starts a right turn, setting into motion the fluid in the semi-circular canal of the inner ear, sending a signal to his brain that he is in a right turn. If he then levels his wings, the fluid in the inner ear is still moving and still sending a signal to his brain that he is in a right turn. The phenomenon experienced is what is known as vertigo.

To the man on the ground it is often called "swimmer's ear", but to the aviator, it is simply a matter of not knowing "which way is up".

If our aviator responds to everything that feels right, everything his body is telling him, he will continue to turn back to the left. If he turns his aircraft with the nose up, he can stall the aircraft, enter a spin and crash and burn. If he continues to turn nose down, he will enter an ever-tightening descending spiral called a graveyard spiral, the end of which speaks for itself. The only hope for our aviator is to ignore what his body is telling him and get onto his flight instruments, the primary instrument of which is his attitude gyro.

The whole intent of the slow turns on the climb out from the field in Meridian was to induce vertigo. Every aviator has experienced vertigo at one time or another. Forget this "seat of the pants" flying. Only by experiencing vertigo and learning to trust his flight instruments over his own feelings can a pilot ensure that he will live to have a long career.

I once thought I pretty much had life figured out. With a value system based on the Ten Commandments and the Golden Rule, I reasoned one day I would come before my Maker, and as long as the good things I did outnumbered the bad, He would say "Fritz, you tried real hard, you did your best, you can come on into heaven." Many today believe as I did. They are experiencing spiritual vertigo. The Bible says in Proverbs 14:12 and Proverbs 16:25(NKJV) "There is a way that seems right to a man, but its end is the way of death." The only hope for man is to get onto his flight instruments and the primary flight instrument of life is the Word of God. Jesus said, as recorded in the Word of God, John14:6(NKJV), "I am the way, the truth, and the life. No one comes to the Father except through Me."

What is your hope beyond the grave? Is your hope based on what feels right or seems right to you?

# ON THE FRITZ

## *"Simply an Illusion"*

The moment that presents the most apprehension for a fighter pilot when operating from the deck of an aircraft carrier is the catapult shot. It is the one time the pilot knows for certain his fate is in the hands of someone other than himself. For my F-4 Phantom, end speed was about ten knots over the stall speed, and one miscue or wrong setting by the catapult crew could result in a "cold cat shot". Since we didn't have an ejection seat with zero airspeed and altitude capability, the only hope for survival would be to try to time an ejection so, as the aircraft slid over the bow of the carrier, the seat would fire you clear of the ship, and you could avoid being run over and caught up in the screws. At any other time, we fighter pilots generally believed our fate was in our own hands. We were driven to try to control everything. If we ever found ourselves in a situation where we couldn't control the aircraft, we simply got out.

I spent most of my young life believing that I was in control and could determine my own destiny. January 31, 1966, was the first time I found myself in a situation where I couldn't control the outcome. Hit by enemy anti-aircraft fire seventy miles inland over North Vietnam, I had lost a major portion of my flight controls and sustained the loss of other critical systems. I had considered the prospect of death before entering combat and quite honestly, I was not afraid of dying. I did, however, have some close friends who had been shot down and captured and were being held in prison camps in Hanoi, and I knew the government was not doing anything to gain their release. If I were captured, I would be on my own, and the thought of being a POW did frighten me. I didn't want to spend a major portion of my life in a North Vietnamese prison camp. For those of you who have heard my story, you know God in His grace did spare me from what I most feared. As a result, in time the outcome changed my life.

Several years ago, I had the opportunity to share my story with the inmates of a maximum-security prison in Midland, Michigan. When I left that prison, I realized that, but for the grace of God, I could have been born the son of a minority single mother on crack cocaine in inner-city Detroit instead of the eldest son of a Caucasian middle-class family in New Orleans. I had no control over the circumstances of my birth and I will have no control over the circumstances of my departure. No one has enough control over his life to add a single hour. "And which of you by being anxious can add a single hour to his span of life." Luke 12:25(ESV). "But as for me, it is good to be near God. I have made the **Sovereign** Lord my refuge; I will tell of all your deeds." Psalm 73:28(NIV). We all like to believe we are in control of our own lives, but I am convinced the idea of control is "simply an Illusion", for God is absolutely sovereign.

So, how about you? Do you believe that that you can really control the circumstances of your life? Have you considered seeking the One who really is in control?

# ON THE FRITZ

## *"Just getting passed over for a promotion and one good hurricane"*

My friend, Lieutenant Colonel Ralph Spencer, USMC, had worked his way up through the ranks, serving his country through World War II, Korea, and Vietnam. While residing in Florida, he concluded that everything in which he had invested his life could be taken away by simply getting "passed over for a promotion and one good hurricane". Growing up in New Orleans, I was familiar with hurricanes, but as I was reflecting on Ralph's words, I couldn't help but think about "Ivan"; no not "Ivan the Terrible" but "Hurricane Ivan". In the fall of 2005, Hurricane Ivan struck Pensacola, and in just one three-month period we suffered personal financial losses from hurricane damage, Delta Airlines declared bankruptcy dissolving my pension along with the rest of the pilot pension fund, and one of my investment managers defrauded the investors' IRAs, stealing major amounts from each of his clients. When I left my accountant's office after discussing my 2005 income taxes, my accountant was literally in tears.

While our unemployment rate today remains high and the real estate market is a disaster, this August we have watched the Dow Jones Industrials take a roller coaster ride and have wondered, "When the dust settles, just where will we find it to be?" This might not be too critical for younger men who still have time to recover, but for those who are "more experienced", our earning days are in their twilight and such fluctuations can be quite disconcerting.

Physical exercise has always been part of my lifestyle and I enjoy working out regularly at the local YMCA. By regular exercise, a nutritious and healthy diet, enough vitamin supplements to choke a horse, and God's grace, I have managed to enjoy extremely good health. However, in spite of all my efforts, I am still unable to reverse the "second law of thermodynamics" and have begun wonder, "who is the old guy looking back at me in the mirror?" I have finally concluded that "if you live long enough, you are going to die."

Again, by God's grace, my bride and I are getting ready to celebrate our golden anniversary, but I discovered years ago, no matter how much you may care for someone, one wrong turn or one slip of the tongue can end the relationship in a hurry. Also, given enough time, everyone will disappoint you. So, if one can't depend on relationships, and if he can't depend on health, and if he can't depend on his job or investments, can he depend on anything?

A constant is something that is invariable or unchanging. Most of us are familiar with a constant as a mathematical term, but in the ever-changing and unpredictable world, I have found my constant in a person. He is immutable, and the Lord Jesus Christ is the same yesterday, today, and tomorrow. Knowing He is my only dependable, I strive to stay close.

So how would you fare in a hurricane? What are you depending on to carry you through the major storms of life and do you have a constant?

# ON THE FRITZ

## *"Just paint the front of the house; forget the rest."*

These were the words of my father, Fred H. Klumpp, one of the youngest men ever to be licensed as a real estate broker. Dad was widely known in the real estate business in New Orleans, and at one time his motto, "A Look Means a Lot", could be seen on for sale signs throughout the metropolitan area. Dad stated those words somewhat in jest, but on reflection, I wonder if they really didn't express much more than simple humor. Outwardly, Dad was very jovial. He was everyone's friend and was always ready with a joke. His dress was immaculate and on the cutting edge; as a fashion trendsetter, he was even written up in the local newspaper. Appearances seemed to mean everything to him. As I grew up, I realized that hidden behind that jovial exterior was a tremendous pain. Raised by second generation American Germans in a dysfunctional home, he learned to anesthetize pain with adult beverages. How many of us can relate; "just paint the front and forget the rest."

Although I didn't consciously adopt Dad's philosophy, like it or not I did become a people pleaser. My image was important, and I made every effort to ensure that what you saw looked good. Underneath that exterior was a person that only God and I knew; one who could be quite different from what I allowed others to see. I have found some books are worth the price just for the title.

"*Why am I Afraid to Tell Who I Am?*" is just such a book, for the title, goes on to say, "*You Might Not Like Me and That's All That I've Got*".

The Bible tells us that not only are we unable to live up to God's standard, but we can't even live up to our own. It took me thirty-two years to finally come to the realization that no matter how hard I tried, I could not in my own strength be the person I wanted to be. "Coming out of the cave with my hands up," I said, "God if I can know You, I want to know You and I am willing to meet You on Your terms." In so many words, God's response was, "It's about time."

Several years later I met a businessman who really impressed me; he was the most transparent man I had ever met. I was so impressed that I prayed a simple prayer, "God make me transparent". If I had known what that would cost, I'm not so sure I would have made such a request, for I had some things in my past I would have just as soon remained hidden.

I have now concluded there is great freedom in living a transparent life. "What you see is what you get." There is no longer fear that someone might one day open a secret closet and my loved ones find I'm not the person they thought I was. Also, there is great accountability; if I would not want the whole world to see what I am doing, I simply should not be doing it.

Have you considered what someone might find if they either walked to your back door or opened your closet?

## ON THE FRITZ

# *"Go Ahead and Take a Mulligan"*

What kind of sport is this anyway? No gouging, no kicking, no punching, no running, no jumping, no wrestling, in fact, no body contact at all. Why you don't even raise up a good sweat. Besides, it takes so much time. I concluded it must be a sport for old men, so maybe when I am old enough and have more time, I might give golf a try.

I have previously written that I determined, "If you live long enough, you're going to die". I applauded myself for such an astute observation, but then also concluded, "If you live long enough you must also go through the process of aging." This process may make some things like a bottle of fine wine better but unfortunately, it doesn't affect the physical body the same way. Approaching three score and ten, I finally decided that I qualified by age, and finding myself among the ranks of the unemployed, I certainly had enough time. So, three years ago, by invitation of some other senior citizens, I finally took up the game of golf.

In spite of the inadequacy of my game, the fellows I regularly play with are out for a good time and exercise a tremendous amount of grace. Time and again, when I either dribble the ball off the tee or slice it into the woods they will say, "Go ahead and take a mulligan." Those words, my friends, are music to my ears. It's not a term you will necessarily hear on the PGA Tour or among the pros, but for us amateur golfers it's a phase we all love to hear. For those unfamiliar with the game of golf, a mulligan means you get a fresh start. Without taking a penalty, you get to hit again.

We all have an innate sense of right and wrong based on the values we develop through our own experience. These can stem from any number of factors including parental influence, education, environmental conditions, the legal system, and religious training. Some people simply allow society and current acceptable cultural norms to determine their personal code of conduct. Our sense of justice, in turn, leads us to believe we will be judged by God based on our adherence to these chosen ethics. The bad news is, if we are honest with ourselves, we have to admit, not only can we not live up to God's ideals, but we can't even live up to our own standards. The good news is God, through His grace, has provided a "Mulligan", and it is simply up to us to accept His provision of a fresh start by faith. "If anyone is in Christ, he is a new creation; old things have passed away; behold all things have become new". 2 Corinthians 5:17(NKJV) "If we confess our sins, He is faithful and just to forgive us our sins and cleanse us from all unrighteousness." 1 John 1:9(NKJV)

What has been the basis for your own personal measurement of acceptable behavior? So how are you doing; to what degree have you been able to live up to your own standards?

# ON THE FRITZ

## *"Do You Love Me?"*

"Do you love me?" she asked. "I'm here aren't I", I replied. I didn't have a clue. I was the oldest son in a male-dominated family and had attended male military schools since the fifth grade. Until I said "I do", I had experienced only short dating relationships and had absolutely zero understanding of how women think. "She is so sensitive", I thought. "Why does she take everything personally? Why can't she be like the guys in the squadron?" Of course, if she had been like the guys in the squadron, I wouldn't have been attracted to her in the first place.

I had always heard that marriage was a fifty-fifty proposition. I envisioned a football field with opposing players on each end of the field. My role was to advance to the fifty-yard line and go no further. It was her responsibility to meet me half way. One problem with such a view is each player sees the fifty-yard line at a different place.

Now don't misunderstand; I did love my wife to the very extent of my capacity to love. However, everything I had learned as a military officer and fighter pilot taught me that I needed to be independent and self-sufficient, so fearing I would become emotionally dependent, when I felt drawn close, I would push away. When I finally agreed to meet God on His terms, I began to read the Bible and I soon realized how much God loved me. I now believe, until one begins to understand how much God loves him or her personally, their capacity to love is severely limited.

Paul writes in Ephesians, "Husbands, love your wives, just as Christ also loved the church and gave Himself for her." Realizing how much God loves me, I desire to follow God's command to love my wife in response to Him. This means loving my wife unconditionally, regardless of her response. God has promised in Hebrews 13:5 that He will never leave me nor forsake me, so it also means I must never leave nor forsake her. Since I have surrendered my life completely to God, I no longer needed to be concerned with protecting myself from rejection or other emotional pain. That is now God's responsibility.

How do I know God loves me? I know because He demonstrated His love in terms I can comprehend. "God so loved the world that He gave His only begotten Son, that whoever believes in Him should not perish but have everlasting life." John 3:16(NKJV) If I am to love my wife as Christ loves the church, I must demonstrate that love in terms that she can understand. Guess what? I find the more I act in love toward my wife, the more I fall in love with her.

Have you ever considered how much God loves you, personally, and how He has demonstrated that love? If so, what has been your response?

# ON THE FRITZ

## *"Not a Chance"*

Invited to speak at the Governor's Prayer Breakfast, I arrived in Little Rock the afternoon before the scheduled event. This event was an annual affair organized by a group of businessmen, and although the Governor was not directly involved, he attended and gave support to the event by granting them the right to use his name. At the time we were living in Atlanta and I didn't even know who the Governor of Arkansas was.

After checking into the hotel, I joined the men who had organized the event for dinner, as was the usual practice. "You will be sitting next to the governor in the morning, so we want you to know a little bit about him." They went on to tell me that he was a Rhodes Scholar and the youngest governor ever elected. After his first term, he was defeated, and now, after being out of the office for four years, he had just been re-elected. He desired one day to be President.

The next morning as we sat together over breakfast, we engaged in just small talk. I initiated most of the conversation, asking questions about his family. He did say he had one daughter and when I asked about his wife, he responded that she was not in attendance.

The governor was introduced and made some opening remarks, after which I was introduced and gave my usual motivational inspirational message centered on God, family, and country. At the conclusion, the MC said: "We usually have a picture-taking session with our speaker and the governor at the Capital, but the governor says he is very busy and can't make it this morning." That wasn't a big deal for me, for I was not there to have my picture taken with the governor.

When I arrived back in Atlanta, Ann asked, "How did it go?' I proceeded to tell her I thought it went well and concluded by telling her the governor said that he wanted to be president one day. "What do you think?" she asked. "Not a chance" I responded.

My purpose in telling this story is simply to point out that we all make judgments based on externals; what we can see or discern from outward appearances. Because people do judge us by what they see, appearances are important and we certainly should give consideration to physical fitness, personal grooming, and appropriate dress, but in doing so we would be foolish to disregard what God sees and what He says is important. What He says is: "People look at the outward appearance, but the Lord looks at the heart. "1 Samuel 16:7(NIV) Just as we take time to look in a mirror, we would be wise to take time occasionally for a little introspection.

Do you give attention only to appearances and what man sees? When God looks at your heart what does He see?

# ON THE FRITZ

## *"Nothing New Under the Sun"*

Being born in the United States and living during the latter half of the twentieth century is a blessing that I have, for most of my life, taken for granted. My earliest memories include air raid drills, victory gardens, rationing stamps, and then, ultimately, the excitement of final victory. It was a great time to be an American, for our nation had liberated Europe and defeated Japan. There was a strong sense of national pride.

Since our laws were founded on a Judeo-Christian value system, we also took pride in the fact that we were a moral nation. Divorce and pregnancy out of wedlock were frowned upon, abortion was unlawful and rare, homosexuality was considered a sexual perversion, and the Ten Commandments and prayer in school was the norm. Bibles were read in public and Christmas was clearly accepted as a celebration of the birth of Christ. The military school I attended reinforced those values. On Saturdays, I watched the Victory at Sea series and decided that serving this nation with a commitment to help preserve those values was a worthy cause. At the Naval Academy, we were expected to adhere to a strong honor code; chapel attendance was mandatory, and upon graduation, we were given a Bible. Somehow, I just assumed that things would continue as they were.

My Vietnam experience, the radical changes of the sixties, and the ensuing erosion of our nation's values led me to question whether this nation as I knew it could survive. For a long time, I hoped things might turn around, but following our last election, I have accepted the fact that this just is not going to happen. I should not be surprised, for King Solomon has written, "That which has been is what will be, that which is done is what will be done, and there is nothing new under the sun." Ecclesiastes 1:9(NKJV) Has any nation other than Israel survived?

My friend, Captain Gus Wenzel, recently brought to my attention a quote from Marcus Tullius Cicero: "Do not blame Caesar, blame the people of Rome who have so enthusiastically acclaimed and adored him and rejoiced in their loss of freedom and danced in his path and gave him triumphal processions. Blame the people who hail him when he speaks in the Forum of the 'new, wonderful, good society' which shall now be Rome's, interpreted to mean: more money, more ease, more security, more living fatly at the expense of the industrious."

Do these changes sadden me? Of course, they do. I am just so thankful that as a follower of Christ, my ultimate citizenship is not here.

Are you someone who has been greatly disheartened by recent changes in our nation? If so, where is your ultimate citizenship? Where is your hope?

# ON THE FRITZ

## *"Peddling Religion"*

At the time, I had ended my Navy career and was flying for Delta Airlines as co-pilot on a DC-8. I had been with the airlines for about six years, long enough for my fellow pilots who knew me to see that something in my life had radically changed. Those changes often prompted questions. It was during the process of answering one of the captain's questions that apparently the flight engineer had overheard our conversation. In more of a question than a statement of fact he queried, "You must be very religious?" Now how do I answer such a question in a way he can understand that it's really not about religion, but rather a relationship?

For years I had embraced a value system that I would have defined as based on the Ten Commandments and the Golden Rule. However, if asked, I could not have even told you what all the Ten Commandments were. If you had asked me if I were a Christian, I would have said yes. I wasn't Jewish, I wasn't a Muslim, and I wasn't a Buddhist. It was more a matter of religious preference, for it certainly wasn't a way of life. In retrospect, it was my own personal religion. If approached on the subject by anyone with any amount of zeal, I would have quickly changed the subject, concluding they were simply peddling religion.

Religions, all religions, are simply man's best effort to reach God. But that poses a dilemma you see because try as he might, a man can't reach God. What is hard for men to grasp is that man cannot do for himself what God, through His initiative, has done for man. If one were to take the personality out of all religions but one, the tenets of the religion would not change. The one exception would be biblical, rather than cultural Christianity, for biblical Christianity is a relationship rather than a religion. It is a personal relationship with the person of Jesus Christ.

Joe Foss, Marine fighter pilot, combat ace, recipient of the Medal of Honor, General in the Air National Guard, Governor of South Dakota, Commissioner of the American Football League, and President of the National Rifle Association, came to a personal relationship with Jesus Christ rather late in life. I remember the interview when a reporter, expecting a deep theological answer, asked Joe what had happened. Joe simply responded, "I was blind and now I see."

So how did I respond to the flight engineer's question? "No, I'm not religious," I said. "I lost my religion when I became a Christian." Jesus of Nazareth said, as recorded in Revelation 3:20(NKJV), "Behold, I stand at the door and knock. If anyone hears my voice and opens the door, I will come into him and dine with him, and he with me."

Do you consider yourself religious? If so, has your religion brought answers to life greatest questions and filled that yearning that every man has in the deepest recesses of his soul?

# *"Purgamentum Init, Exit Purgamentum"*

The inscription on my new t-shirt, a birthday gift from my daughter, read in big bold letters, "**PURGAMENTUM INIT, EXIT PURGAMENTUM**". Beneath that inscription in smaller red lettering it read: "GARBAGE IN, GARBAGE OUT". How many times had my children heard me state those very words as I attempted to influence what they watched on television or at the movies, or the music they listened to and what they read?

Growing up in New Orleans in the fifties, during the birth of the rhythm and blues and rock and roll era, I learned to love all kinds of music. However, many years later, as an airline pilot driving home after an all-nighter and listening to country music, I realized the powerful impact the words of the song were having on my emotions.

The human mind is a wonderful and extremely complex computer, but like any computer, what comes out is no better than the value or validity of what is programmed in. We begin receiving data while still in our mother's womb and continue receiving input throughout our lives. These data shape the way we think as we develop our world view. Our world view determines our values and our values, in turn, influence our behavior. Many of us go through life without ever considering the validity of those things that have influenced our thinking.

My friend, Captain "WOW", said, "I feel pretty good Fritz

until I pick up my morning newspaper. When I begin to read it, I get very angry and depressed". My response was: "Then why do you read the paper?" Denis Waitley in "*Seeds of Greatness*" writes that all one need do, to be fully informed, is read the news summary on the front page of "The Wall Street Journal".

Until I began to read what God had to say, I too had never taken time to examine what had influenced my thinking. Paul of Tarsus has written in Romans 12:2(NKJV), "And do not be conformed to this world, but be transformed by the renewing of your mind, that you may prove what *is* that good and acceptable and perfect will of God." With all of the written media, television, and the internet, we live in an era of information overload. I am constantly being bombarded with all kinds of data. If I am to maintain clear thinking, my challenge is to determine what of all of this information is valid and based on truth. In order to make that determination, it is necessary for me to ensure I am programming my computer with what I know to be true. Jesus said, as recorded in John 14:6 (NKJV), "I am the way and the truth and the life."

So, what has shaped your thinking? Are you programming your computer with what you believe to be true and if so, what is the basis for your belief?

# ON THE FRITZ

## *"A Very Special Weekend"*

September 8, 2001, was a very special weekend; the 40th reunion of our Naval Academy class. Every ten years we gather on the banks of the Chesapeake, renew friendships, tell sea stories, and just enjoy time together. One of my classmates was Bud Flagg. As young fighter pilots stationed at NAS Miramar in San Diego, Bud and I would share rides to the base and leave our other automobile for Ann and Bud's wife Dee. We soon moved on to different squadrons.

Following deployments to Vietnam, we both made the decision to leave regular naval service and join the airlines. Bud went to work for American Airlines and I went with Delta. Unlike me, however, Bud continued in the Naval Reserves and had an extremely successful career, eventually rising to the rank of Admiral. During these years, the only time I would see Bud and Dee was at the reunions. At our 40th, I had recently retired from Delta and Bud, having retired from the Navy and the airlines, was living on a horse farm in northern Virginia.

On Thursday evening we met for cocktails and to catch up. On Friday, as was customary, we gathered in Memorial Hall for a service honoring our fallen classmates. Then it was on to the parade grounds where we were honored guests for the parade of Midshipmen. It was a glorious fall day. As the Brigade marched by under a clear blue sky, I could see the spinnaker sails billowing on the sailboats on the Chesapeake. Saturday, after a tailgate party at Navy-Marine Corps Memorial Stadium, we saw absolutely the worst football game I have ever seen as Navy lost in record fashion to Georgia Tech. Since I had a business meeting in Detroit, I left shortly after the game. I saw Bud and Dee for the last time at the tailgate party before leaving for Detroit on Sunday and then home on Monday.

At home on Tuesday, 9-11, I watched the tragic events of that fateful day. The following morning, I received an e-mail from another classmate, Admiral Skip McGinley. Skip wrote that as he was driving into work, he saw the American Airlines 757 hit the Pentagon. He went on to say that Bud and Dee were aboard that aircraft. All of those things that had recently seemed so important- those decorations Bud had received for his time in combat, that gold braid that he wore on the sleeve of his uniform, the awards for his successful airline career, his IRA, and the horse farm- on Wednesday, September 12, none of them mattered. The only thing that mattered was who was Jesus Christ to Bud personally. "And this is the testimony: that God has given us eternal life, and this life is in His Son. He who has the Son has life; he who does not have the Son of God does not have life. These things I have written to you who believe in the name of the son of God, that you may know that you have eternal life." 1 John 5:11-13(NKJV).

We will all experience a "9-11", either corporately or individually. My question is when your "9-11" comes, where will you be on "9-12"?

## ON THE FRITZ

# *"I Resolve"*

As we begin the New Year have you once again resolved to do some things differently? Are your New Year's resolutions the same ones you made last year? Have you decided those didn't work, so you should try something completely different? Or have you just decided to quit trying altogether? I have heard it said, the reason New Year's resolutions fail is that they are based on what we think we should do rather than what we want to do. If this is so, then is there anything we can do to resolve our dilemma and bring the things we "want to do" into alignment with those things we feel we should do?

Since I believe our behavior is a reflection of our values and our values are derived from our world view, in my opinion, it is futile for someone to try to modify their behavior without first examining their world view or core beliefs. I tried to change my behavior for years and do what I thought I should do. As hard as I tried to be the person I thought I should be, my best efforts ended in utter frustration. It wasn't until my world view and my values changed that eventually my behavior slowly began to change.

Most serious New Year's resolutions usually involve overcoming a destructive or harmful habit, modifying spending and getting out of debt, diet and exercise, or reading and studying for self-improvement. At least this was the case for me. So, are there core values that speak to each of these particular issues, and if so, from where are they?

The major change in my core values occurred when I "came out of the cave with my hands up", and surrendered my life to Christ. As I began to read and study God's Word, my values changed. Before long, my behavior began to change. So how does God's truth speak to these particular issues? As far as debt, the Bible says "the borrower is the slave of the lender." Proverbs 22:7(ESV). When considering diet and exercise or destructive habits, I am reminded that my "body is the temple of the Holy Spirit within me." 1 Corinthians 6:19(ESV). What source of study for self-improvement could I possibly find that is greater than the one given by the very one who created me? "Study to show yourself approved of God, a workman that need not be ashamed, rightly dividing the word of truth." 2 Timothy 2:15(KJV)

# ON THE FRITZ

## *"Sincerely Wrong"*

Because of the weather, our refueling stop at Iwakuni Marine Corps Air Station required a high-altitude instrument penetration. The carrier had departed Yokosuka, Japan for the South China Sea. My orders were to wait for one of our squadron Phantom fighters to complete maintenance procedures at Atsugi NAS, and then rejoin the carrier south of Taiwan. The refueling stop was necessary prior to the long overwater portion of the trip.

I reduced power, lowered my nose, and began my instrument approach. Since my descent rate, as indicated by my altimeter, was less than expected, I reduced the power to idle. The weather was forecast high overcast and I had been in instrument flight conditions since well before the start of my approach. Although I had never flown into Iwakuni, I knew there were mountains in the area. The slow movement of the altimeter continued to indicate a slow descent. Suddenly my altimeter began to rapidly unwind and as my pulse rapidly increased, I knew I had been receiving erroneous altitude information. We suddenly broke out of the overcast and could see mountains all around. We were then able to visually complete our landing. Our erroneous information was the result of pitot icing because of a faulty heater. We have recently read of major aircraft accidents that could have possibly been attributed to this very same thing.

Pilots know how critical it is to be right and how unforgiving mistakes can be. My friend Kirby Sumner was very sincere, when he flew his F-4 into the ground during a practice instrument approach at Pt. Mugu Naval Air Station. He believed his altimeter was indicating one altitude, when in reality it was indicating another. He was flying under the hood during instrument training. His aircraft burned on the runway. As they were putting him in a body bag, they realized he was still alive, and although he was horribly burned, he did survive.

When asking others what they believe concerning their eternal destination, I get a variety of answers. I never question their sincerity, but do wonder if they have taken an honest look at why they believe as they do. Sincerity is no substitute for truth. In this case, a mistaken belief can have eternal consequences. They can be sincerely wrong.

A number of years ago I was with a friend and we were discussing the loss of his fortune. Fred Steenmeyer had turned his contracting business over to another, and retired to Hawaii. The business was to provide the funding for his retirement. When the new owner declared bankruptcy, Fred lost everything and needed to return to Anchorage. As we discussed his loss Fred said with a smile," Fritz, just remember we stake our destiny on Jesus Christ." This very same Jesus said, "I am the way and the truth and the life. No one comes to the Father except through me." John 14:6(NKJV) Once again, sincerity is no substitute for truth. If I am wrong, I will have lost nothing. If those who place their hope on something else are wrong, they will have lost everything.

So where is your hope? On what or on whom have you placed your faith?

ON THE FRITZ

# *"True for You, But Not for Me"*

"True for you but not for me"? I was stunned that this pilot could possibly believe that truth was subjective and simply based on what one feels is right. How could an airline captain make such a statement knowing that his life, as well as the lives of his passengers, are dependent his ability to make correct decisions based on absolute truth? Often, as when dealing with an in-flight emergency or flying on instruments during a low visibility approach, there is absolutely no room for error. Nonetheless, I have found that he is not alone. We live in a culture where more people than not, believe that there are no absolute truths and everything is relative.

Years ago, my friend, Col. Nimrod McNair, said: "Fritz, the principles of business that Harvard Graduate School of Business teaches that actually work are scripturally based." He went on to say that it doesn't necessarily mean that Harvard Graduate School knows that, and they teach many principles that don't work. Nonetheless, "truth is truth no matter where you find it", and if one applies those principles, he should expect certain results. I have never forgotten my friend's words and over the years by observation, I've put his premise to the test.

For thirty years I worked for a company that I believed had been blessed with good management. In time I realized that their success could be attributed to the fact that they operated on three basic principles; stay out of debt, take care of your people, and take care of your customers. Whether they knew it or not these principles are biblical. Unfortunately, the last CEO before my retirement changed course, and as he systematically abandoned these principles, the fortunes of the company fell. This eventually led the company into bankruptcy.

It has been very enlightening to observe leadership at all levels, whether it's a husband and father guiding his own family, or a president or CEO providing leadership for a major corporation. The ones who apply biblical principles achieve a certain level of success. It really makes no difference what their personal beliefs are, or what their position is in regard to religion. Once again, "truth is truth no matter where you find it". On a personal note, I can honestly say that most of the failures and grief that I have experienced can be attributed to the violation of principles and precepts that are either clearly stated or can be inferred by example from the Scriptures.

When asked by Pontius Pilot, Governor of Judea, if he were a king, Jesus of Nazareth replied, "You say rightly that I am a king. For this cause I was born and for this cause I have come into the world, that I should bear witness to the truth." John 18:37(NKJV) Pilot, in turn, replied, "What is truth?" John18:38(NKJV)

Have you considered the importance of believing there is absolute truth when determining whether something is true or not? What reference do you use in defining truth?

# ON THE FRITZ

## *"So, what is next?"*

From the moment I first met Horatio, I was totally captivated. C. S. Forester's Horatio Hornblower made an indelible impression on me. I can't remember exactly when it happened, but Horatio became a constant companion, and as I shared in his adventures, I concluded that the greatest adventure for a young man was to go to sea. In fifth grade, I wrote a paper in which I stated that my goal in life was to go to the Naval Academy and eventually rise to the rank of Admiral. What could possibly be more meaningful than a life filled with adventure?

Ten and a half years from the day that I took the oath of office as a Midshipman, U.S. Navy, my resignation was accepted. I departed my last duty station an angry and disillusioned young man. Our nation's "no win policy" in Vietnam was committing men to combat without giving them the means to win. The war was being micromanaged from the White House by the President and his Secretary of Defense, and military leaders were not even allowed to make tactical decisions, much less strategic decisions related to the conduct of the war. I had many close friends and classmates who were being held prisoners in Hanoi and we were not doing anything to ensure their release. I felt betrayed by my country and my Commander-in-Chief. I had experienced high adventure, but adventure alone was not enough.

When I entered the Navy, I knew that I would never make

much money, but material wealth for me was irrelevant. Once I departed the Navy, however, I decided that if I couldn't be an Admiral then I'd become a millionaire. I looked for every opportunity to make a buck. In just a few years I was enjoying more material success than I had ever considered, but the more I had the more I wanted, and I finally concluded whatever was missing in my life, it couldn't be satisfied with material things.

Intent on trying to help change a world that appeared to be spiraling out of control, I got involved in grassroots politics with the intent of seeking political office myself. Once again, I became disillusioned, for I saw that once men gain political office, they make decisions based upon their own personal interests, rather than doing what is best for the nation at large.

If adventure and material wealth can't satisfy, and political power can't provide fulfillment, then what can? So, what is next? Blaise Pascal, a French physicist and philosopher said, "every man has a God-shaped vacuum." Men and women seek to fill that vacuum with all sorts of things, but since that vacuum is God-shaped, they eventually discover, just as I had, nothing else can fill that void. God alone can fulfill man's deepest yearning.

So, what have you been using to try to fill that void in your life? Has it left you wondering what is next?

# ON THE FRITZ

## *"The best is yet to come"*

"If I am going to keep my head above water, I need to hear everything the professor is saying." I don't recall which engineering class it was, but I do remember that I was having a tough time. Looking over to my left I noticed that Paul was sitting there writing music. It was then I realized that he was operating on a whole different plane. Paul Robert Kleindorfer, affectionately known by his Naval Academy classmates as Moose, is one of the brightest men I have ever known. Arriving at the Naval Academy from North Judson, Indiana, Moose distinguished himself not only in Academics, but on the athletic field, Glee Club, Choir, and Concert Band as well. In spite of his accomplishments, many of us remember him best for his good nature and a fantastic sense of humor.

Following graduation, Moose took a commission in the Army. Ann and I had the pleasure of a visit from him in Pensacola where I was going through Naval Flight Training. Moose was going through Special Forces training at Eglin Air Force Base. That was the last time that I would see Moose for many years.

Today, Moose, or more appropriately Dr. Kleindorfer, is Distinguished Research Professor in Technology and Operations Management at INSEAD, the Business School for the World. He is Professor Emeritus of Management Science at the Wharton School of the University of Pennsylvania and has held university appointments at Carnegie Mellon University, Massachusetts Institute of Technology, the Wharton School and several universities and international research institutes. He has published over 25 books and many research papers. His accomplishments are way too many to enumerate here.

The last time I saw Moose was at the fifty-year reunion of our Naval Academy Class. It was then that Moose informed us that he has Lou Gehrig's Disease. Since he and his wife are living in Paris, it is not easy to keep up with the state of his health, but he recently gave us an update via e-mail. The terrible disease has taken such a toll that he is now dependent on others for his most basic needs. He ended his up-date by simply saying, "The best is yet to come." I don't know if I have ever been more deeply moved or inspired than I was by those words by Moose at this particular time. Only a man who knows God can speak of his future with such certainty.

"And this is the testimony: that God has given us eternal life, and this life is in His Son. He who has the Son has life: he who does not have the Son of God does not have life." 1 John 5:11,12(NKJV). In God's economy, there are really only two kinds of people, and in the end, it is not our accomplishments, but only our relationship with Christ that matters.

If you were in Paul's shoes could you say "the best is yet to come"? If not, why not?

ON THE FRITZ

# *"What Can I Possibly Say?"*

As I stood there in Arlington National Cemetery by Terry's graveside, I had asked myself many times the days before, what can I possibly say that will bring comfort to Terry's family and at the same time bring hope to those Naval Academy classmates and friends who had gathered to honor his ultimate sacrifice?

It had been many years since Terry was reported missing in action during the first aerial combat engagement of the Vietnam War. At the time, Terry had become perhaps, of my Naval Academy classmates, my closest friend. Although we were assigned to different air groups and deployed on different carriers, we maintained a close relationship. He was deployed while my squadron was stateside, and when his squadron returned, I tried to find out what had happened. Because of the sensitive nature of the incident, it was classified secret and I was unable to get answers. I had dreamed for many years that Terry was still alive.

Through the Freedom of Information Act, Terry's daughter, Helen, had been able to get sufficient information to determine Terry was no longer MIA, but finally declared dead. Although his remains were never recovered, full military honors were scheduled and a casket was to be interred at Arlington. I had helped her in a small way and that is why she had asked me to speak at the graveside on behalf of the family.

"If Terry could be here", I began, "he would say something

so ridiculously funny you could not help but burst out laughing. That's just the way Terry was. He was always joyful and no matter how hard or dire the circumstances, he would have something to say that would cause others to laugh. When you consider his tragic death at such an early age one cannot help but ask why? I don't think my God minds that we ask why, but this side of eternity there are many questions the answers to which God chooses to remain silent."

"You may find it very difficult to accept a God who chooses to remain silent. Perhaps I would too until I consider the nature of the God who chooses to remain silent. Then I remember it is a God that loves me so much, He was willing to come to earth in the form of man, to be ridiculed, spat upon, and beaten by men, and die a horrible death. All of this to take upon Himself the punishment for my sin and rebellion against God. When I consider this, I can accept the fact that God chooses to remain silent."

This Christmas I reflect in absolute wonderment at the miracle of the incarnation. Although I cannot fully comprehend it, I accept it. ""Behold, the virgin shall be with child, and bear a Son, and they shall call His name Immanuel," which is translated, "God with us." Matthew 1:23(NKJV)

# ON THE FRITZ

## *"Why do I do what I do?"*

"You look pretty good", my high school track coach said; "If you just wouldn't run so long in one place." Like the man in a rocking chair, there was a whole lot of activity, but not much progress. So, if I have been so busy, what have I accomplished? If I have accomplished little, why do I continue to do what I do?

During the last few years, I have been fascinated with the life of one who has been known as the wisest man who ever lived. Solomon, son of David and Israel's third king, reigned during the tenth century BC. He ruled during Israel's golden age and his achievements are absolutely amazing. Yet in spite of that, his summation, as expressed near the end of his life and recorded in the Book of Ecclesiastes, is "all is vanity". Looking at Solomon and all he accomplished I cannot help but ask, "How could one who started so well and did so much, come to the end of his life and conclude that everything that he accomplished is meaningless?"

Many of us idealistically start out doing something that we feel will give meaning to our lives, but in time become disillusioned. I believe this is the case with many who begin their careers in the military. The realities of war, however, can lead to disillusionment, and the resulting loss of purpose can even contribute to PTSD. The same disillusionment can be experienced by those engaged in politics or the workplace.

Everyone wants his life to count for something, and we all desire to live a life of meaning. I have previously discussed the "God-shaped vacuum" that exists in the heart of every man; a vacuum only the Lord can fill. John Maxwell in "*The Maxwell Leadership Bible*" speaks of another vacuum; the life-sized vacuum inside one's heart that only a life mission can fill.

According to Ecclesiastes, Solomon's conclusion that "all is vanity and grasping for the wind" pertains to works done "under the sun". If a meaningful purpose in life cannot be found "under the sun", then we must look elsewhere; we must look to the heavens. If we are to find real meaning and purpose, we must look to God Himself.

My friend and mentor, Joe Coggeshall, challenged me for many years to write a "life purpose statement". Successful companies have a purpose statement", he would say, "so why don't you?" I finally took his challenge to heart and have since found that my written life purpose has become a compass allowing me to forsake the good for the sake of seeking the best.

So, what is your purpose and why do you do what you do? Do you have a life purpose statement? If not, why not?

# NORTHLAKE CHRISTIAN SCHOOL

## *A Vision Fulfilled*

In the late spring of 1972, as God's remnant in the Covington area boldly preached His Word, His Spirit began to move in a powerful way. This outpouring of the Holy Spirit resulted in revival and recommitment for some, and spiritual awakening, conviction, repentance, and regeneration for many others.

As a result of this movement, during the summer of 1972, home Bible studies sprang up throughout the area. From these Bible studies, a group of men, under the leadership of Rudy Adkins, banded together to form Tammany Christian Fellowship. The purpose of Tammany Christian Fellowship was to seize the opportunity to saturate the North Shore community with the Gospel of Christ. The original officers of Tammany Christian Fellowship were: Glenn Young- President, Stuart McClendon-Vice President, Fritz Klumpp- Secretary, Kirk Triplett- Treasurer, and Rudy Atkins- Executive Director. Additional charter members were Jim Simpson, Don Watson, Bruce Southerland, Bob Thompson, Sam Camp, Jim Holmes, Pete Hendry, William Schenck, C.W. Smith, Billy Graham, Hank McGrew, Gerard Verkaik, and Terry Goodger.

It was in the wake of this revival that God began to plant the seed of a vision. I felt the need for a school that would be an extension of the values that we were teaching our children at home. The only one that I knew that had any knowledge of

Christian education was Stuart McClendon. Stuart had children who attended Ben Lippen School in Asheville, North Carolina. I shared my dream of a Christian school with Stuart and found that Stuart shared the same dream.

A dream without action remains only a dream. Action without a dream is merely busyness. A dream with action becomes a vision, so Stuart and I began to pray for a Christian school, and a speaker was invited into the area to meet in several homes to discuss Christian education. The next step was taken in the spring of 1979 when Ron Hunter, Stuart McClendon, Steve Jahncke, Jim Saucier, and I met to discuss the next step. After much discussion and prayer, we decided to trust God to give us a new Christian school, kindergarten through twelfth grade, which would open in the fall of 1979. We had no money, no building. no curriculum, no faculty, and no students. We did have the vision for a school that would provide a college preparatory education based on biblical principles as a service to Christian families and a testimony to the entire community. I was elected Chairman of the Founding Board, Stuart McClendon was named Secretary, and Steve Jahncke, Treasurer. I ordered a book on starting a Christian school from a church in Indianapolis, Indiana, and the search for facilities, faculty, students, and curriculum began.

It was determined that the school would not be affiliated with any particular church or denomination. The founding board wanted to ensure that the school is viewed as a ministry to the entire Christian community. Godly men from differing churches caught the vision and were invited to join the board. The school board met almost every week during that first year, and many hours on weeknights and Saturday mornings were spent in corporate prayer.

After the search for a church that would consider rental of

their education facilities proved futile, Pete Hendry generously offered the use of his veterinary hospital. He had just completed the construction of a new building, and the old facility, consisting of a small house, a garage, and a garage apartment, was to become the site of Northlake Christian School. A church associated with Tammany Christian Fellowship had already begun to meet in the house, and a Christian bookstore, which had been opened in the garage, was moved and the garage became the kindergarten. The apartment above the garage became the administrative offices, headmaster's office, and faculty lounge. The house was used primarily for the elementary grades, and a new doublewide trailer housed the high school grades and was also used as an auditorium. The transition was made from the auditorium to the classroom by the use of folding tables and chairs. Desks that were destined to burn by the Tammy Parish School Board were bought for $1.00–$1.25 apiece and refinished by the Klumpp family in their carport during the summer months.

Teachers were recruited from friends and families associated with Tammy Christian Fellowship. Some had teaching degrees but most did not. They did, however, have college degrees, a love for God, and a desire to be used by Him. Dave Diamond and Marlene Flot were members of the initial teaching staff.

The board, during a visit to Pensacola Christian School to inspect their school and review the A-Beka curriculum, was introduced to Gordon Carlisle. Gordon was at that time on staff at Pensacola Christian. Gordon subsequently was invited to Northlake Christian School as headmaster and arrived in Covington in time to fill the remaining faculty positions and complete the curriculum selection for the coming school year.

Many prospective students viewed attending a new school as an enjoyable adventure, but to most of the high school students, the visit by the chairman, Fritz Klumpp, to their parents for the purpose of recruitment, was as appreciated as a visit from the Gestapo. Most parents were concerned about accreditation and had to be convinced that they were not sacrificing their child's future for college admittance and education. On the opening day of Northlake Christian School, 110 students were seated at their desks.

Volunteers from enrolled students, students' families, and friends labored together the last two weeks before school, and in those two weeks, the veterinary clinic and garage were transformed into the campus for Northlake Christian School.

During that first year, we had a full athletic program and fielded a flag football team, girls' and boys' basketball and softball teams, and had a cheerleading squad. At the first graduation ceremony, NCS awarded high-school diplomas to five graduating seniors; Jim Gauley, Frank Graziano, Chip Block, Joan Adkins, and Judy Hunter. Each of the graduating seniors continued on to a university.

By the start of the second-year, enrollment had increased to 170 students. Gordon Carlisle transferred to the junior-high faculty staff for the 1980-81 school year and Stuart McClendon took time away from his law practice to serve as headmaster for most of the second year. Steve Jahncke filled the headmaster position for the balance of that year.

The search continued during this time for a permanent school site, and during the year Jim Simpson gifted a portion of land adjoining his sod farm. The location of this property was deemed inappropriate for the permanent site, but the proceeds from the sale of this gift provided the funds that were eventually used to construct the first classrooms on the permanent site. Donald Kearns was part owner of a sixteen-acre tract of land located near the Tulane University Primate Research Center. He was instrumental in arranging the sale of the property at a price that was fully paid for by the sale of the existing timber on the property. Thus, God provided the site for the present campus of Northlake Christian School.

By the third year, NCS had classrooms constructed through the services of Terry Goodger and paid for by proceeds from the sale of the land gift from Jim Simpson. NCS started the third school year with an enrollment of 210 students, located on a campus of sixteen acres, and had absolutely no indebtedness. I then passed the chairmanship of the NCS Board to Walter Jahncke.

Northlake Christian School stands today as a testimony to God's grace; "**A Vision Fulfilled.**"

The following was written for the bride of my youth to whom, with our three children, this book is dedicated. The poem depicts our journey together from our first date, a beach party, to the present. Each verse speaks of a different step in our pilgrimage.

### To the Captor of My Soul

*A starlit night on a golden isle*
*An unknown stirring of the soul,*
*Along the shore a tender kiss*
*I did not walk alone.*

*Bold words spoken from a heart*
*Stirred to move to worlds unknown,*
*Boyhood dreams fulfilled on a day in June*
*I did not walk alone.*

*Down the aisle of commitment where two became one,*
*The thrill of new life, the fruit of young love,*
*Golden wings in the Texas sun*
*I did not walk alone.*

*Through the valley of the shadow of death*
*Illuminated by bursts of fire and smoke,*
*Home again to waiting arms*
*I did not walk alone.*

*Wandering aimlessly*
*Amid hopes unfulfilled,*
*Stumbling onward a desperate lonely soul*
*I did not walk alone.*

Drawn by the grace of a loving God
Reaching out to one confused and lost,
Through the gates of eternal life
I did not walk alone.

The joy of a heart set free to learn
To love the captor of his soul,
A new direction and a path defined
I did not walk alone.

Time to restore a love long lost,
New beginning more solid than the first,
A time of healing sparking fires afresh
I did not walk alone.

It is autumn and winter comes too soon
A life of passion with my bride of youth,
To streets of gold, we will soon move on
We will not walk alone.

Printed in the United States
By Bookmasters